99 Classroom Calamities . . .
How to Avoid Them

CW00342910

99 Classroom Calamities . . . And How to Avoid Them

Or: How to Survive in Teaching Beyond Your Training

Tabatha Rayment

continuum

Continuum International Publishing Group

The Tower Building	Suite 704
11 York Road	80 Maiden Lane
London	New York
SE1 7NX	NY 10038

British Library Cataloguing-in-Publication Data
A catalogue record for this book is available from the British Library.

ISBN: 0–8264–9157–X (paperback)

Typeset by Servis Filmsetting Ltd, Manchester
Printed and bound in Great Britain by
MPG Books Ltd, Bodmin, Cornwall

This book is dedicated to David, Melanie, Graham and Sue,
with special mention to my darling Benjamin

With huge thanks to all the wonderful teachers
who shared their opinions and stories

Contents

Being Part of the Team

Finding Support

Assessment and Feedback

Getting Out

Staying Put

A Few More Classroom Calamities

The Beginning Stages

Introduction – why write this book?

This book was written for a very important reason. Contrary to what the title may suggest, it was not written to put people off the idea of becoming teachers. (In most cases, the general media does enough to put people off the idea of teaching, more than any book could!) This book was written to enlighten and to entertain, to tell the truth about what it's like to be a teacher, and to help you survive beyond your training years.

There are hundreds of books on the market that will help you to plan, assess, organize and evaluate, but very few tell you about the real problems teachers face: problems that have very little to do with how they perform under observation or how they have developed their teaching portfolio. How would you cope with a wasp in the classroom, organizing a field trip or difficult relationships with colleagues? This book looks at what it can be like to be a teacher as a person, not just as another cog in the education machine.

In short, this book tells you the truth about day-to-day teaching. Rather than focus on the academic side of teaching life, it looks to the personal side, and asks real teachers how they feel about their profession. More than that, it will tell you what no one else does – 99 classroom calamities, and how to avoid then!

Notes

The term 'parents' refers to whoever is the primary carer of the child in question.

The quotes and anecdotes included in this text are the real opinions of real teachers. Some names have been changed at their request.

Understanding the icons

Throughout this book you will find some handy icons that are used to draw your attention to key areas in the text. The light bulb icon denotes a helpful tip or explains something you may find useful to remember.

The exclamation sign denotes a warning or highlights something that you should be aware of as a teacher.

1 So you want to be a teacher?

People choose to become teachers for a variety of reasons. Maybe they have had fantastic experiences in classrooms, or have a real love for teaching and learning. Some wish to find a new career or further an existing one. Others simply do it for the money!

There are many different teacher training options, just as there are many varied reasons for deciding to train in the first place. Whether you are still at school or college, just about to leave university, or whether you have been working for a while and wish to change your career path, there is a training option for you.

New recruits can expect to receive financial funding to help them afford the cost of training. Postgraduates can obtain a tax-free training bursary from £6,000 to £9,000, with the potential of a 'Golden Hello' of up to £5,000 once they finish their induction. A starting salary for a Newly Qualified Teacher (NQT) with Qualified Teacher Status is around £19,500 per annum.

The adverts you may have seen on TV show teaching as a challenging yet highly rewarding career with competitive salary rates. Teachers are portrayed as incredibly dedicated and organized individuals with clear goals and unique career paths, who spend their days engaging and motivating the youth of today. There is some truth in these images: but there is also another side to teaching that isn't so widely broadcast.

Teaching is not easy; in fact many new teachers are quite taken aback by how hard it can be. Their dreams of short hours, long holidays and excellent pay are often soon thwarted by the reality of lots of hard work, the almost total disappearance of free time, and meeting some truly nightmarish classes.

So why do perfectly sane individuals choose to become a part of the madcap world of the teaching profession?

I chose to be a teacher because of my love for English, and because the experiences I had while working in a sixth-form college made me realize how much I enjoyed working with children. My best friend saw teaching as the most logical employment route to take with an Art History degree. Although our reasons were rather different, they didn't have any bearing on our enjoyment of the work.

Below are some reasons real teachers gave for choosing the teaching profession:

I finished university with an engineering degree and ended up getting a job as a driving instructor. I wanted to find a job that was more than just a job, and made me feel like I was actually using my degree for a change. I ended up applying to teach secondary mathematics and haven't looked back since.

Dave, Mathematics teacher (32)

I have an English degree and was teaching a part-time creative writing course for adults for quite a few years. When it became apparent that I was going to lose my job I decided I wanted to keep on teaching and decided to get a professional qualification to teach Literature at A-level.

Karen, English Literature teacher (56)

I had always wanted to be a teacher, but I ended up getting married and having children instead of going to university. My husband and I separated, and as my kids were older I decided to apply to a university as a mature student. I got my degree and went on to take a PGCE course.

Sharon, English and Drama teacher (48)

I always thought I would end up working with children, and I did some work experience in a child-minding group. I thought about being a child-minder for a while, but then I thought that teaching might be more fun. I took a Bachelor of Education course and went on to teach at my old primary school!

Sarita, Primary teacher (26)

To be honest, I was stuck in a rut in my old job and was looking for something new. I saw the teacher training adverts on television and decided to give it a shot and apply. It meant I could look forward to a new career and leave my old one with minimum fuss. I can't for the life of me think why I didn't go into teaching first of all, I love it.

Luke, Modern Foreign Languages teacher (29)

2 First impressions really matter

Scientific studies claim that within the first five seconds of meeting a new person, they will have made evaluative judgements about you – even if that initial encounter is nothing more than a quick glance.

Whether or not that statement is true, there is no doubt that students are remarkably efficient in sizing you up at your first meeting. It seems that within only a few minutes, many of them will have already figured out what kinds of things annoy you the most, and how best to make you snap. Perhaps it is due to some strange, student sixth sense that we eventually lose as adults.

Every new teacher, whether experienced or new to the profession, should be aware of the high level of importance surrounding first impressions. Shuffling into the classroom with your head down, shoulders hunched and a terrified expression on your face is not going to endear you to more hardened members of your class. You will become nothing more than a moving target. Surprisingly, I have seen an awful lot of teachers do this, even experienced ones.

Regardless of how petrified you may feel, you must always enter a class with your back straight, your head held high and a face that shows keen determination. You must be like the 'Terminator' of teaching. As the character, Reese, says in the movie:

> 'Listen. And understand. That Terminator is out there. It can't be bargained with. It can't be reasoned with. It doesn't feel pity, or remorse, or fear. And it absolutely will not stop, ever, until you are dead.'
>
> *(The Terminator: James Cameron, 1984)*

Perhaps that might seem a little over the top, but when it goes wrong, it can *really* go wrong.

> I had been a supply teacher for about six weeks. I knew I was a pretty good teacher, but I was a bit too shy. My friend told me to alter how I approached my initial meetings with classes, claiming that a confident teacher gets more respect.
>
> On Monday morning I strode purposefully into the classroom, with my chin up high. Unfortunately, I completely failed to notice the cable of the OHP stretched across my path, and ended up flat on my face in front of my new class. Unsurprisingly, for a good few weeks afterwards, my attempts to gain more respect fell similarly flat.
>
> *Sarah, Humanities teacher (27)*

Remember: however scared you may feel inside NEVER let it show on the outside. Always ensure that any messages you give out through your body language project an image of total control and self-confidence.

3 **Making it clear what you expect**

Following on from first impressions is the setting of initial ground rules. Every teacher has his or her own personal ground rules, and some are fiercer or more lenient than others.

 Be aware: never automatically assume that your class already knows the rules – you must be the one to tell them.

Ground rules put you in charge from the start. They allow you to lay down the law and make it clear what you will and won't put up with. More than that, they help you to make some instant evaluations of your class. How they react and respond to your ground rules often signifies how they will behave in general.

Have a handy list already made up for your first meeting, and display it in a prominent place. Give each student a copy if you feel you need to. Make sure everyone understands your rules, and stick to them rigidly. There is no point having a great set of ground rules that go out of the window within the first three weeks.

Continuously assess and reaffirm your ground rules to make sure you are getting the best out of them. Adopt a policy of 'my classroom, my rules' and don't be persuaded to change your mind.

'Ground rules are invaluable things. I was advised to have a 'rule chart' when I first trained as a teacher, and I have had one ever since. It acts like a contract between my class and me and we all know where we stand with each other. If they are being particularly rowdy I don't even have to say anything, I can just point to my rules chart and they know that's their cue to calm down.'

Geoff, Head of Year 7 and Design Technology teacher (35)

7

4 Who's that girl?

Remembering names is never easy. On an average school day, one secondary teacher may have taught anywhere between 120 to 180 students, depending on school class sizes. Primary classes can be a little easier, as in most cases the students stay with one teacher throughout the year: but you may still be expected to be on first name terms with most of the children in the school.

So how on earth do you remember them all?

Seating plans can be very useful, as students will be seated in the same place every time you see them (see Calamity 5 for more information), but it can be tedious to have to keep referring to a diagram all the time.

A colleague of mine used to put little notes in her register such as:

Smith, James Gordon – *very small/ginger hair*
Wilson, Rebecca Jane – *lots of freckles/very noisy*

However, she almost suffered disaster when one of her students happened to be reading over her shoulder one day and asked her why she had written, 'looks like Woody Allen' next to his name. Apparently, the child had reminded her of the Hollywood director. She had thought it was a relatively harmless comment. The child's parents, however, did not fully agree!

Instead of writing notes, try to store that information in your own head, and practise naming the students silently when they enter your room or you see them in the corridor.

Some students will be more memorable than others – usually it is the noisy, naughty ones you will remember the most! However, there are some students' names you always forget, no matter how many times you teach them.

Sneaky ways to remember names:

- Ask students to make name tags and put them at the front of their desks when they come into the class for the first two or three weeks.
- Keep a close eye on who answers to which name when taking class registers – if in doubt, get students to raise their hand as well as calling 'here'.
- Take note of any defining features that might help you remember a student.

- Use a seating plan and stick to it until you have learned all the new names.

- Stand at the door and greet each student as they come in to practise names. Those students you forget will therefore be frequently offering their name.

- Make sure you are the person to give books out for the first few weeks, to practice getting to know who's who.

- Look for clues surrounding the student, e.g. if their name is written on their exercise book or pencil case.

- Repeat the name to yourself and connect the face to the name in your head. The next time you see the student you should be able to visualize their name more easily.

- Students tend to stick to groups. Sometimes you can remember the group easier than the individual, and figure out who's who by a process of elimination.

- Link names to features or characteristics, e.g. Ginger James or Tall Paul. Sometimes you might be able to link names to celebrities: for years I thought of one girl as Posh Spice, simply because her name was Victoria Benson.

And finally, make sure you get the name right from the start.

A rather poorly behaved student in my class told me his name was Daniel Stephens. For almost two weeks I had been handing out detentions and admonishments to the boy. Eventually, the real Daniel Stephens came to ask me why I had given him a detention, when I didn't even teach him. Needless to say I felt very silly indeed.

Louise, Science teacher (28)

5   Getting 'em where you want 'em

Seating plans can be brilliantly helpful things, or they can be more trouble than they are worth. They can help to sort out who should go where and also to remember names of new students, but it's not always easy getting students to stick to them.

When meeting a class for the first time, I will always let them sit where they want. In that first meeting I can judge straight away who should be kept well away from whom! Usually, the best way to begin a seating plan is to sit every student alphabetically, and boy/girl as far as possible. However, I have been responsible for some budding romances in my classes through this method, which isn't always helpful!

An alphabetical boy/girl start can help you figure out who works well with each other, and who should probably be kept apart. With regards to less well-behaved students, you only really have two choices. You can either put them at the front so you can keep an eye on them – but end up having to talk over them sometimes; or you put them at the back out of the way – but where you can't always see what they get up to! Personally, I prefer to put them at the front where I can keep a close eye on them when necessary, but can also choose tactically to ignore them when they are being a real pain!

You don't have to stick to class lists for a whole year. I know teachers who have kept their class seating plans for long periods of time, only to lose any possible benefit from them as students get to know each other better. Sometimes it is more helpful to mix them around a bit and keep things a surprise.

 As a final point, just like Calamities 4's advice of making sure you have the correct names, always make sure you are the one to fill in any seating plans. Students are remarkably crafty when it comes to duping you, and before you realize it, you may end up with a rigid class seating plan of your student's devising, rather than your own!

6 Respect my authority!

The old adage tells us that in order to earn respect, you must show respect. However, sometimes it may seem that someone forgot to inform today's students of this fact.

Even if you have been in the profession for over 20 years, the people who will be impressed by this achievement are not the ones you will be standing in front of and teaching. Never assume that just because you had Class 3B eating out of your hand, that Class 4A will react in the same way. Mutual respect and control of the class are two tricky things.

An assertive teacher should be able to create a positive and productive atmosphere in a classroom environment without resorting to potentially hostile behaviour. This means ensuring you are in control from the very moment you enter the room. Establish ground rules, set clearly defined seating plans and walk into the classroom as if you alone are the ruler of the class.

This is usually far easier to do with classes of younger students: in fact, the older the student range, the scarier the initial meeting can be. There is no shame in admitting that many Year 11 classes frighten you witless!

Gaining respect and control are two things you must do before you try to do anything else. If students suspect you are meek and mild, it is a sad fact that it's very likely that they will walk all over you. However, gain a reputation as being a bit of a dragon, and you are more likely to find that you are merely disliked and distrusted.

Top tips for gaining respect and control

- Walk tall – always enter the classroom looking like you mean business.
- Be firm but fair – make it known early on what you will not tolerate, but don't put yourself across as a monster!
- Deal with problems quickly and quietly – stamp out any unwanted behaviour as soon as it arises, but don't make a big deal out of it.
- Get on their level – establish that you have control of the class, but don't talk down to your students: treat them as equals as much as possible.
- Call by name – learn and remember your students' names and use them regularly.
- Be seen outside your classroom – become an integral part of the school. Take time to talk to students at break, lunch and outside of school. Be seen as a person as well as a teacher.

7 Picking up where others have left off

Taking over someone else's class can happen at any time. Whether you are new to the school, teaching supply or doing cover lessons, at some point you may have to take over where another teacher has left off.

Cover lessons and supply are generally easier to deal with. Usually you will have been left some lesson material, and all that is really required of you is to teach it and look after the class. If you are a new teacher, or are taking over a class halfway through a term, you may find more problems.

Initially, taking over someone else's class is a bit like going to Manderley, the house in Daphne du Maurier's novel, *Rebecca* (1938). You will be constantly compared to those you replaced, and they will always have done whatever it is you do much better.

You can either be content to work in someone else's shadow, and continue as they had started, or you can break away completely and start afresh – either approach works amply as well.

The top five tips for taking over someone else's class

1   Remember, it's your class now – regardless of whether you are covering for someone else, or you have inherited the class on a permanent basis, you are in control of the class. Just because the students constantly remind you of 'but Mr Johnson lets us do it . . .' doesn't mean you have to conform.
2   Make your mark – whether that is by establishing ground rules or launching straight into the teaching, gain your position at the head of the class.
3   Don't change too much too soon – if you do decide to change the way things are done, go slowly. Making too many major overhauls will be unnecessarily stressful for you and your class.
4   Do some research – where possible, take the time to find out about the class and give yourself some ideas on what to expect. Check out past grades, behaviour reports and exercise books.
5   Ignore the ghosts – wherever possible, stay clear of making reference to your predecessor, and definitely do not criticize them, even if they have left things in an awful mess for you! Don't make yourself paranoid wondering if you are better or worse than they were: be confident in your own skills and abilities.

Organizing Your Time

8 Not enough hours in the day – Workload pressures

Teachers don't get much free time. Forget long holidays and short working days, teaching is a very demanding and tiring profession. All my non-teaching friends seem to think I'm exaggerating when I say I haven't stopped all day.

I understand why: they haven't seen me travelling to school at seven o'clock on a winter morning, trying to ensure I get into school on time. They aren't there when I give up my Sundays to mark a stack of Year 8 essays. They definitely haven't seen me during my badly-named 'free' period, when I am chasing up missing students, getting my photo-copying organized, locating 34 copies of *Macbeth*, telephoning Tommy Smith's mother and herding a bunch of rowdy teenagers into assembly! On top of all that I have my usual stack of planning and preparation. Sometimes it can feel like there just aren't enough hours in the day.

Unfortunately, until human cloning becomes commonplace, these are the things that teachers have to find the time to do. There are some teachers who seem to genuinely enjoy being on the go all the time. While I love teaching, I certainly don't love it enough to devote every single waking moment to it!

Teaching can be an exhausting and demanding profession, and it is a completely unique kind of working environment. It does take a couple of years in the business before you can really grant yourself the odd truly free period, and even then you must be prepared to put in the hard work to get good rewards. This means accepting that some days you are going to be on your feet and busy all day. All teachers every-where have to do it, even those hardened and experienced individuals who have taught for 30 years and can re-use old lesson plans when they need to.

9   One hour to plan ten lessons

Since September 2005, all teachers in the UK are legally entitled to 10 per cent of their timetable as non-contact time. This is more commonly known as Planning, Preparation and Assessment time (PPA). The idea is that this gives teachers guaranteed time to do their necessary PPA tasks.

However, if we break this down mathematically:

One average secondary school day = 6 lessons.
One full timetable = 30 lessons per week.
10% of 30 lessons = 3 lessons per week.

Three lessons to plan, prepare and assess a potential 27 lessons isn't an awful lot of time. Particularly if you teach a core subject, 'free' lessons are sacred things.

> I have a 'shrine' to my free lessons. Inside this shrine is my timetable, stuck to my office wall behind my desk with my 'free' lessons carefully highlighted in luminescent yellow marker pen. When I am asked to use one of my 'frees' to cover a lesson, I have been known to get rather grumpy!
>
> *Rick, Physical Education teacher (34)*

There is a saviour available in the form of the wonderful Educational Planner – your class list, diary, planning aid and mark book all rolled into one. If your school does not provide you with this, buy one for yourself! Planners should never travel home with you; they should stay in your room all the time. This means, if you are absent or late, any teacher can flick through your planner and know what you have taught to date, and what you plan to teach.

Regardless of teacher age or experience, a planner can be a godsend when you need to quick-fix four classes in ten minutes. Just a few pencilled-in lines that give a brief idea of what direction the lesson should take is often all that is needed.

 Remember: Your educational planner is an incredibly useful teaching tool – always use your planner!

10 Timetable woes

An average teacher's timetable runs from 9 a.m. to 3.30 p.m., Monday to Friday, and is divided up into roughly six lessons per day. This means a teacher could theoretically be teaching 30 sessions a week.

Thankfully, this very rarely happens, and we do get some free time in which to do our other necessary teaching obligations. However, in most cases, the timetable can become rather unbalanced. Some days are utterly jam-packed, while others have perhaps only two set lessons.

The temptation to use the easy days to 'slack off' can be quite high, especially if the easy day happens to fall on a Friday afternoon. **Don't do it!** Teaching might not be a usual 9 to 5 job, but it will certainly help you to keep on top of things if you view it that way.

Aim to work a full 7.5 to 8 hours a day; no more and no less, if you can. This also means you can switch off when you get home. Use your time at school to do school-related tasks. Try not to take marking and planning home, but do it before or after teaching hours. This way schoolwork stays at school.

 Remember: if you feel like your timetable is too busy (or even too sparse), have a word with your Head of Department and find out if things can be moved around.

11 This isn't my class!

There will come a time when you are asked to cover someone else's lesson. This can be a daunting task for any teacher, whether you are a permanent member of school staff, or a supply teacher from an outside agency.

Cover lessons are usually best if they are simple and don't require you to teach too much about a subject you are unfamiliar with. They are even better if they have already been planned by someone else!

Top tips to survive a cover lesson

Before the students arrive:

- Make sure you know where you should be, what lesson you're covering and what class to expect.
- Sort out a class list or register and find out where exercise books, paper, pens, and other equipment are kept.
- Get there before the students and read through any notes or lesson plans that have been left for you. If anything seems too confusing, don't attempt to teach it. You will only end up confusing the students too!
- Greet the students at the door and seat them where *you* want them, not where *they* want to be.

At the beginning of the lesson:

- Introduce yourself – even if the students already know who you are. Explain why you are in the classroom. If necessary, write your name on the board.
- Take a class register.
- Use the notes left by the usual teacher to explain the lesson's aims and objectives. If necessary, write them on the board.
- Do not apologize for not knowing the subject material – never admit you're out of your depth. Remember, you're in charge.
- Check that the whole class understands what they have been asked to do.

During the lesson:

- Keep checking that pupils are following the task set, just as you would in your own lessons.
- Do not use a cover lesson as an opportunity to mark work or read a book – treat cover lessons with the same importance as your own lessons.
- If there are any problems, write them down. This includes names of poorly behaved students or any undesirable incidents. Later, pass this information on to the teacher you are covering for.

At the end of the lesson:

- Leave the classroom in a clean and tidy state. Make sure all books and equipment are put back where they belong.
- Ensure that any notes or lesson plans are left in the classroom – don't take them away, as others may need them for subsequent sessions.
- Dismiss the students in an orderly manner.

12 Keeping free periods free

Free periods are sacred things. It is important to keep a close eye on them, otherwise they seem to disappear like magic! Before you know it, your free periods have become cover lessons, marking sessions, department meetings and photocopier marathons.

 Be aware: their name is a misnomer; a free period suggests that you have free time, but that is very rarely the case, and to be fair, it should never *be* the case! As tired as you may be, free periods are not to be used as opportunities to drink coffee and read newspapers in the staff room!

What should a free period be used for?

- Any activity associated with your teaching duties such as planning, marking, organizing, finding resources, writing reports, etc.
- Department meetings, planning and discussions appropriate to your teaching subject.
- Cover lessons as required by the school – within acceptable limits.
- Additional study sessions as required.
- Observation of other teachers or team teaching activities.

What should a free period NOT be used for?

- Disappearing off to the staffroom for a coffee/tea/sneaky cigarette break.
- Unauthorized departure from the school grounds for shopping trips, pub visits, hairdresser's appointments, etc.
- Constant covering of lessons – you are entitled to your 10 per cent non-contact time to plan and prepare.

This does not mean that you can't use ten minutes of your free period to grab a coffee or take a brisk stroll around the school grounds, but do remember that you are a professional and have many working obligations to fulfil.

In my early days as a teacher I would often end up in the staffroom, nursing a cup of coffee and attempting to get stuck in to my marking. Unfortunately, everyone always seemed to try to talk to me or distract me, and I never got anything done. Now I always stay in my classroom with the door firmly locked so I can get on with some work. I still grab a coffee though!

John, Humanities teacher (36)

13 Managing your time

Good time management is all down to being organized. It's no good expecting your students to do their homework on time, if you haven't done yours. However, sometimes you may have extra demands placed on you which may make you feel as if you are expected to be in lots of different places at once.

 Be aware: it is essential that you prioritize your work-load and ensure that you are setting realistic timescales. If you are spending all your waking hours doing nothing but teaching, organizing, marking and planning, then something needs to change.

If problems are arising thanks to senior management piling on more and more work, then don't be afraid to speak up. If you are being asked to stretch yourself too thin, remember you can say no! It can be a good idea to accept a little extra paperwork now and again to show you are willing and dedicated, but be aware that if you keep accepting it, it will fast become expected of you.

Delegate your workload and your time with your colleagues. Instead of taking too much on and subsequently spending your time rushing frantically around the school, only take on as much extra work as you can realistically manage.

 Remember: don't be pushed into doing things you don't really want to or haven't the time for. Coffee breaks don't have to be a luxury!

Effective time management tips

1 Set yourself specific goals.
2 Prioritize and economize.
3 Use a 'to do' list.
4 Spend time planning and organizing.
5 Learn to say 'no'.
6 Delegate and eliminate.
7 Be flexible.
8 Prepare for the unexpected.
9 Focus on effectiveness and efficiency.
10 Give yourself rewards.

Planning, Preparation and Paperwork

14 You make it look so easy

New teachers have to be observed to pass their QTS and NQT, but how about when the experienced teacher being observed by a student or professional is you?

Teacher observations are important as they allow for opportunities to:

1 Identify strengths and weaknesses in an individual's teaching style.
2 Help prepare for external observations and teaching assessments.
3 Make formal judgements about teaching ability and quality.
4 Self-assess teaching ability and address problem areas.

Taking a keen interest in your own and others' teaching will help you to expand your skills, and assist colleagues to expand theirs.

 Be aware: never allow yourself to fall into complacency, or even worse, fool yourself into believing that after 20 years of teaching you can't possibly learn anything new. There will always be new styles and techniques to pick up on and adopt into your own teaching methodology.

Preparing for an observation

The following are key areas an observer will be looking for. You can ensure you have a successful observation session by taking some time to consider these points yourself.

1 Are your learning aims and objectives clear?
2 Do you have a good relationship with your students – do they respond well to you?
3 Are you confident in your teaching and subject knowledge?
4 Have you done adequate planning and organization for the lesson?
5 Have you organized any additional learning materials to use in this session?
6 Is your teaching and learning methodology appropriate?
7 Is your delivery and pace appropriate?
8 Do you actively encourage your students to learn and participate?
9 Are you making good use of your physical surroundings and resources?
10 Do you constantly and consistently monitor and assess your class?

Always make sure you get feedback from your observer, and discuss how you thought it went. A pair of outside eyes may pick up on areas you have missed, or perhaps they may have some useful criticism to help you improve.

 Remember: never get defensive or feel upset about a poor observation; the most important thing is that you use the feedback to improve and assess.

15 If you have nothing nice to say . . .

One of the most tedious, and sometimes the most difficult, tasks of teaching is writing reports. All teachers have to do it, and sometimes it can be hard to think what to write. Whatever you write on the report card will stick with that student, potentially for a long, long time. Allegedly, even people who have had a substantial impact on others' lives, such as Sir Winston Churchill and Princess Diana, once received poor school reports.

Regardless of how unenthusiastic you feel about writing reports, they are essential to student progress, monitoring and assessment. A six-word comment isn't going to tell anyone anything much, and will only make it look like you are disinterested or couldn't be bothered. Imagine how you would feel if you had put lots of effort into a business project, only to receive feedback that merely said, 'Good progress. Some nice work.'

Top tips for writing reports

- Consider how many reports you will have to write. It is likely that you will have to write a comment for every child you teach, not to mention additional ones if you are a form tutor or head of year. You might end up having to write comments for over 200 students! Organize your time efficiently – don't spend any longer than a few minutes on each one.
- Keep comments positive and refer to achievements.
- Avoid generalizations – be specific and concise.
- Do not refer to the student's personality – focus more on their academic progress.
- Offer ways to improve or progress rather than criticize.
- Always be honest and fair.
- Make sure you consider content and presentation.

Remember: Keep reports positive and truthful. If you can't find anything nice to say, don't say anything at all!

20 useful phrases for report cards

- *Has performed very well in . . .*
- *Has an excellent attitude/good temperament.*
- *Is highly motivated/responsible.*
- *Is pleasant and helpful.*
- *Has made considerable improvement in . . .*
- *Is an excellent team player/Works well with others.*
- *Has worked very hard in . . .*
- *Shows a lot of promise.*
- *Shows real interest and enthusiasm.*
- *Is consistently progressing in . . .*
- *Is a conscientious worker.*
- *Is mature and reliable/Is especially confident in . . .*
- *Follows directions/instructions well.*
- *Has made a real contribution to . . .*
- *Participates well in conversation and discussion work.*
- *Shows a positive attitude to learning.*
- *Is independent/self-reliant.*
- *Is eager to learn/Concentrates well.*
- *Is organized/efficient/driven to succeed.*
- *Is particularly creative/Shows real originality/clarity of thinking.*

16 Keeping department records

Every teacher should be familiar with the amount of paperwork that is necessary in the job. Even a daily register is a department record, and it is essential that they are completed properly.

 Be aware: many teachers do not realize that class registers are now used as legal documents, especially when proving cases of truancy. With the law now able to impose fines on parents whose children do not attend school, it is imperative that the records are accurate.

Assessment and monitoring records are also essential documents. These should be legible and concise, and contain enough detail to be useful without being overly cluttered.

How to keep on top of departmental records

- Ensure that all daily records (such as registers) are completed on that day and that the data is forwarded to the relevant department.
- Find out about and learn how to use any relevant electronic data management tools (e.g. PARS, SIMS, and Nova-T).
- Keep clear, legible and concise records detailing important student attainment levels: test scores, grades, reading ages, etc.
- Keep back-ups of everything – paper copies and electronic ones. Ensure that important records and data are saved regularly.
- Any notes or letters received from parents should be saved in a specific file in case they need to be referred to later. Never simply slip them inside your register: they will get lost.
- Medical records, behaviour plans, SEN details, etc. contain confidential and sensitive material – ensure that you treat this information with the care it requires, and be aware of your legal responsibilities when using this information.
- Keep your marking and assessment up to date at all times – you may be asked to produce it unexpectedly.

17 Confused by the curriculum?

Since the government and Education Minister are constantly assessing the UK curriculum, it is inevitable that some changes will occur. Your department may decide to make significant changes to resource materials or alter teaching strategies. If you haven't been keeping up to date, or have returned to teaching from a period away, it is essential that you familiarize yourself with current teaching and learning trends and expectations.

When the curriculum changes, for whatever reason, it is up to you to be familiar with the material you teach. There is no point sticking stolidly to tried-and-tested lesson plans if they are not satisfying curriculum criteria.

In the UK the Qualifications and Curriculum Authority (QCA) is sponsored by the government Department for Education and Skills (DfES), and helps to maintain and develop the National Curriculum.

The QCA supply curriculum frameworks to every school for every subject. An in-depth breakdown of these frameworks can be found on the National Curriculum Online website, www.nc.uk.net, which is available to everyone. (This is not to be confused with Curriculum Online, www.curriculumonline.gov.uk, which contains a wide variety of multimedia resources to support teaching and learning.)

Top tips for following the curriculum

- Are you aware of which section of the curriculum your school is following?
- Are you familiar with skill descriptors for your subject area?
- Have you considered the lesson's expected objectives and outcomes?
- How can you link your lesson to National Curriculum standards?
- Have you adapted your teaching and learning styles to accommodate changes to the subject structures?
- Do you know what level your class is at in comparison to national expectations?
- Are you aware of which exam papers you should be teaching towards?

Remember: if you are confused about any aspects of the curriculum, it is always best to check with your Head of Department or other colleagues to make sure you get it right. Otherwise you may find yourself creating lesson plans that are inappropriate or fail to match proper standards. This is not only a waste of your time, but you will be failing your classes by not teaching appropriate material.

18 Scared by SEN

A lot of students in mainstream schools have Special Educational Need (SEN). In previous years, SEN students were separated from the mainstream: but this is now discouraged as much as possible.

A child is considered to have SEN if he or she has a learning difficulty that requires special educational provision. Although many children may have learning difficulties, a child will be added to a school's SEN register if the difficulty is seen to be significantly greater than the majority of other students of the same age. SEN children will be educated in mainstream schools provided that:

1   They are being provided with the educational provision they need.
2   Any provisions that need to be made do not interfere with the education of others.
3   The resources and provisions needed are available within the school.

Teaching SEN students will mean using some strong inclusion strategies, and differentiation techniques to ensure that every child has access to the same standard and quality of education experienced by their peers.

Tips for teaching SEN students

- Take the time to find out what impact the child's SEN has on his or her learning ability. Find out their strengths, weaknesses and background, etc.
- Never assume that a SEN will automatically create a learning barrier.
- Adapt your teaching style to suit the student – don't expect them to adapt to you.
- Seat SEN students near to the front of the class to help them focus their attention.
- Engage them in the lesson by asking them questions within their ability – make them feel involved.
- Encourage group work so that every child can learn from each other – allow SEN students a little bit more freedom to work with whom they feel comfortable.
- Give written and oral instructions for all activities – ensure the student knows what they have to do and is following the lesson.

- Repeat yourself or approach things in different ways if the student does not understand – be patient.
- Break up each task into small, manageable chunks.
- Differentiate your learning resources so that every student's needs are met, SEN or otherwise.
- Explore how ICT can help SEN students e.g interactive white boards, computer use, and literacy and numeracy support software.
- Where possible, ensure that projects and assignments are skills based and that they are relevant and exciting to the learners.

 Remember: Teaching a SEN student does not need to be a scary prospect. Although you may find it a test of your teaching skills in some ways, it is also a good opportunity to address issues such as differentiation in your teaching and assess how you can make your lesson delivery accessible to all.

19 When the whole school is watching

Assemblies can be scary things, whether you have to organize them, speak in them or just patrol them: if something goes wrong it can be a terrible place to be when the entire school is watching you.

Assemblies don't have to be religious: in fact, a lot of schools have moved away from religion-orientated assemblies in order to cater for the diverse ethnic cultures found in many schools today. Rather than focus on collective worship, many schools now use assemblies to tackle contemporary issues.

Most assemblies only last for roughly 15 minutes, so there is not much scope to go into detail about a topic. Assemblies should be focused, topical, interesting, informative and educational.

Successful assemblies should be planned as carefully as lessons. When planning an assembly, always consider the following questions:

- What is the assembly about?
- What age group of students will you be addressing?
- What message do you want to give to your students?
- How will you convey that message?
- How will you make sure the assembly is relevant and accessible to your students?
- What kind of visual/musical/spoken aids will you use?

 Remember: one of the best ways to get inspiration for assemblies is to keep a close eye on current affairs and the news. Try to use real issues that students will be able to identify with, and help them begin to take more interest in the world around them.

Top ten ideas for school assembly topics

1 Have a 'thought for the day' and read a story connected to this thought.
2 Ask students to read a poem and put on a small drama piece to accompany it.
3 Put on a puppet show to tell an important story.
4 Use comedy to make talking about a difficult topic much easier.
5 Ask a teacher to show off one of their 'hidden talents' (magic show, memory skills, origami, etc.)

6   Copy a television quiz show like *The Weakest Link* or *Who Wants to be a Millionaire* – this is not only fun, it can be used to present ethical issues such as bullying and gambling.

7   Show a short piece of film to highlight a moral or ethical dilemma, and discuss it.

8   Read an article from a national newspaper and discuss the contents.

9   Get everyone involved in singing and/or making music.

10 Interview a 'celebrity' (a student or member of staff dressed up!).

20 Getting lumbered with the classes you hate!

Some classes are truly awful; you hate the students, you're bored by the lesson content and you're stuck with them for a whole three terms. Unfortunately, you can't just pick and choose the classes you want to teach, and ignore those that you don't. However you feel about a particular class, it is up to you to remain professional at all times. Instead of dreading your least-favoured classes, do as much as you can to make your times together fun and educational.

If you really do hate a particular class, be aware that it is highly likely you are giving off 'hate vibes' which your students will pick up on. Emotions can be contagious. Any hostility you have towards the class will only be mirrored back towards you. Not only that, perhaps if you stop and consider *why* you hate the class, you may find that it is really only a few individuals who annoy you the most, rather than the entire bunch.

Keep yourself sane and happy by always putting a positive spin on things. Remember:

1   A professional is a skilled practitioner and expert. Always remain focused and conduct yourself in a professional manner, regardless of how you may feel inside!
2   It is easy to get angry and wound up. It is much harder to remain calm and clear-headed. Don't succumb to negative emotions just because of a few, silly individuals. Always focus on the positives and the 'good' members of the class.
3   Don't harbour grudges; start each day and each lesson with a clean slate. Especially do not take a personal dislike to individuals – however much they might wind you up.
4   If it is the subject content that is making you stressed out, ask for help and advice from other teachers who are teaching the same or similar subjects. Try to find new and different ways of teaching a 'boring' subject. Don't forget, if you're bored by what you teach, your teaching styles are no doubt boring too. This in turn will equate to a very bored, and most likely disruptive, class.
5   If you have been lumbered with the class due to supply or cover duty, keep in mind that they are not your usual class, and that after a specific time period you can walk away and forget them!

I had a terrible time with one of my Year 9 classes, and there were times when I disliked all of them. Whatever I did, my lessons always seemed to go wrong, and they seemed determined to charge around the classroom every time I saw them. One afternoon when it was really sunny, I decided I was sick of being stuck inside with them and took them all outside to sit on the grass to read *Romeo and Juliet*. They absolutely loved it, and were calm all lesson. It was a turning point in our 'relationship'. I only wished I'd done it much sooner!

Marian, English teacher (39)

21 Unsuccessful lessons

Not all lessons go completely to plan. As Robert Burns says in his poem 'To A Mouse' (1785):

> The best laid schemes o' Mice an' Men, gang aft agley.

Regardless of how many hours of careful and meticulous planning we put into our lessons, we should always expect the unexpected.

To a new teacher, lessons that go wrong can be something of a blow to self-esteem and confidence. Most experienced teachers have either got used to things not going to plan, or have worked out ways to prevent mishaps.

 Remember: regardless of how good, experienced or organized a teacher you are, you cannot always prevent a lesson going pear-shaped!

Lessons go wrong for many reasons. The following factors all have an effect on how successful a lesson can be:

- Teaching ability
- Strength of planning
- Teaching styles
- Behaviour
- Subject material
- Subject knowledge
- Environment
- Equipment
- Technology
- Unexpected events

Tips for when a lesson goes wrong

- Never be afraid to stop what you or the class are doing and try a different approach if the lesson simply isn't working. It might be that you have aimed too high or too low, or the subject material simply isn't suitable for that class. Attempting to struggle on with an obviously unsuccessful lesson is merely a waste of time to your students.

- Monitor and assess the situation – has the lesson gone off target due to behaviour issues, or a lack of stimulating material, or have you simply not explained things properly? Never assume that just because you have planned every single, tiny detail that the reality will play out as you imagined.
- Be willing and prepared to accept the 'blame' if a lesson fails, but don't be too hard on yourself. Just because you didn't manage to complete all the tasks on your lesson plan doesn't mean you have completely failed. Think about what went well and what went wrong and work on that in the future.
- Sticking rigidly to a lesson plan is not always a good idea. A good teacher knows how to adapt and be flexible in relation to the demands of the class. Try to view lesson plans as a bare-bones structure, rather than a precise military operation!
- If the lesson has deviated from its intended lesson structure, but the class are engaged, focused and learning, let them carry on! However, try not to let this happen too often. You will find your timing and pace is affected, and it will be difficult to complete any long-term lesson goals.

22 Terrible lessons

Following on from 'Unsuccessful lessons', terrible lessons are when something major goes wrong. When a lesson goes from unsuccessful to terrible, you can be sure that you could not possibly have planned to prevent it.

Different teachers will have very different views on what makes a lesson terrible – this could range from the subject material, to poor planning, to the actual students in the class. However, the primary defining factor of a terrible lesson is that absolutely no learning has taken place.

From minor disruptions outside the classroom to the latest technology 'crashing' around your ears, there will be times when you are best to cut your losses and accept that you are simply not going to get anything done that lesson.

 Remember: while attempting to soldier on is very commendable, it does only lead to more stress in the long run. Don't be scared of shelving your lesson plan and putting things on hold. After all, you cannot teach successfully in a disrupted or discontent environment.

The following tips are for emergencies. When a lesson goes completely down the proverbial toilet, and there is nothing you can do to save it, try some of the following.

- Always keep calm – whatever the situation, there is nothing to be gained by a panicking teacher.
- Keep the best control of the class that you can – try to ensure that pupils stay in their seats and the noise level is kept to a sensible limit.
- Make it very obvious that although the lesson may not be continuing as expected, you are still in control of the class and as such you expect to be listened to and obeyed as necessary.
- Engage the class in other ways. Don't concentrate on the problem, but think about the solution.

Some examples:

Why it has it all gone wrong	What you can do about it
Class left without a teacher (staff shortages) or no cover lesson materials left.	Merge two similar classes if possible. Look to current affairs debating skills. Encourage the class to participate in a discussion based on the subject being studied.
Room issues mean that the class has nowhere to go.	Utilize other rooms in the school such as the dining or assembly hall, or even go outside if the weather is good.
Exams, fire-bells, field trips, etc. have considerably shortened the lesson unexpectedly.	Amend your lesson plan accordingly so that key areas are used – remember, even the simple task of reading a book improves literacy, concentration, spelling and grammar skills.
There is fighting or very bad behaviour in the classroom.	Attempt to separate the class as much as possible so that those directly involved can be dealt with. Get back-up if needed and keep other students away from those who are fighting or misbehaving.

Treat any truly terrible lessons as a learning curve, so that you know what not to do if ever there is a next time!

 Remember: you are only human, and as such you cannot prepare for every eventuality all the time – keep a few tricks up your sleeve so you can address problem areas swiftly and confidently.

23 'There's a wasp in the classroom, Miss!' – Unexpected disruptions

Every so often a lesson you thought was going to be absolutely wonderful ends up becoming a complete farce. Even 20 years of experience can't save you when on one hot day in June you find yourself with an unexpected addition to your classroom – a wasp.

Without warning, a carefully planned and organized lesson turns into a cacophony of voices, flailing arms and students leaping out of their chairs. There is no point using your tried-and-tested behaviour management techniques on this particular disruptive individual, they really will fall on deaf ears. Your behaviour training didn't tell you how to deal with this!

When a lesson falls foul to the forces of nature, there is only one thing you can do: stay calm and attempt to regain control. In any lesson, regardless of how confident and organized you are, all good teachers know to always expect the unexpected.

Strange things do happen in lessons, and sometimes it is impossible to plan for these eventualities. Remember, you have a role to play and, just like any situation in the classroom, you need to keep calm, deal with the problem and then move on as quickly as possible. Never let small problems become major issues: just let them be a test of your professionalism and learn from the experience.

After all, recounting your tale in the staffroom about the dastardly wasp sure beats talking about marking schemes.

Ten unexpected things that can totally disrupt a lesson

1 Wasps, bees, flies and any other kind of uninvited bugs in the classroom.
2 Stray dogs on the playing field.
3 Health-related problems and accidents: nosebleeds, sickness, diabetic/epileptic fits, etc.
4 Unexpected visitors: staff, students, parents, etc.
5 Technology/equipment failures.

6   Passing wind and burping.
7   Arguments and fighting in the classroom or corridor.
8   Trips to the toilet.
9   Fire drills.
10   Workmen and renovations around the school.

Feeling Blue

24 Less shout, more squeak

Most teaching students and NQTs end up losing their voice in the first few months – but even experienced teachers do too.

Teaching puts a huge strain on your vocal chords. No great surprise when you consider how much you use your voice in your profession. Many teachers do not realize that they could be doing lasting damage to their voice, and believe that a husky voice or dry throat is a normal and acceptable hazard of the job.

Top tips to look after your voice

1   Never, ever shout. Not only does shouting put strain on the voice, it is a poor strategy for classroom management. Once you start shouting you have nowhere else to go!
2   Drink lots of fluids to keep your throat well lubricated.
3   Rest your voice whenever possible. Use non-verbal signs to pupils to reduce the use of your voice and ensure that your class stays focused on you.
4   Vary the speed and tone of your speech. Speaking quickly increases tension in the vocal chords.
5   Speaking clearly does not necessarily mean you need to speak loudly. If you address your class quietly they will have to concentrate more on you to hear what you are saying!
6   Your posture is important – stand up straight and look forward. This also projects your voice, meaning that you don't need to raise the volume so much.
7   Avoid eating too many dairy products. Dairy products such as milk and cheese encourage the production of phlegm, which interferes with the natural working of the vocal chords.
8   Even teachers who take good care of their voices may lose them occasionally. When the cold bugs strike, and your voice goes, it can make for some interesting events in the classroom.

 Remember: if you're really struggling because of a vocal loss, it is best to take some time off and rest. Coming to work when you're poorly is never a good idea, but never risk permanently damaging your voice.

In my first weeks as an NQT I caught a rather nasty cold. My voice had started to suffer a little bit, but I didn't want to take any time off as it was a new job and I wanted to make sure I made a good impression.

During the course of the day I ended up getting more and more hoarse. The kids found this hilarious, and took every opportunity they could to play up, knowing I couldn't shout at them. The deputy head came past my classroom during a lesson. It was absolute chaos, and my efforts to make myself heard over the din resulted in nothing but alternate squeaks and croaks. I ended up getting sent home by the deputy head and told off for not looking after my voice!

Vanessa, Art teacher (34)

25 Tummy troubles

None of us are immune to getting ill every so often, and working in a school means exposure to a great deal of germs and viruses. Thankfully, the longer you work in a school, the stronger your immune system will get, until eventually those coughs and sneezes that seemed to plague you forever when you first started teaching become a hazy memory.

However, you should always beware of the other nasty surprises that can sneak up on you. Food poisoning or tummy troubles are difficult ones to avoid sometimes. Observing rules of basic hygiene will help, but what can you do if the tuna sandwich you bought from the canteen at lunchtime ends up backfiring on you?

I'd forgotten to pack my lunch the night before, like I usually did, and I didn't have much choice but to grab a sandwich from the newsagents over the road from the school. They only had egg-filled ones left. Normally I wouldn't really eat eggs, but I was hungry and wanted something fairly healthy. A couple of hours later I knew I'd made a terrible mistake. I was teaching hockey to a class of Year 8s when I started getting the most awful pains in my tummy. I tried to soldier on, but it was no good. With 20 minutes left of the lesson to go, I passed wind very loudly indeed and had no choice but to run off the pitch to the nearest loo. For weeks afterwards I had to put up with some rather unflattering nicknames. I haven't eaten an egg sandwich since!

Catherine, Physical Education teacher (32)

Tips to help avoid any embarrassing health-related incidents

- Packed lunches are usually better than canteen or store-bought lunches, and they're cheaper too. Make sure you store any perishable items in a cool place, and always wash your hands before you munch!
- Keep a supply of handy pills and potions in your bag or a lockable drawer. Painkillers and indigestion tablets are the most commonly required items.
- Avoid eating spicy or unusual foods at school. Lunchtimes are not the time to be trying out a local delicacy!
- If you do eat out at lunchtime, pick places with a good reputation or where you have been before.

- Passing wind and belching aren't advisable things to do in front of your class – if it's really unavoidable to do either, excuse yourself! However, keep in mind you are only human – you might have to put up with a few sniggers and some nicknames, but most students will understand if you're poorly!

Never:

- Try to 'struggle on'. If you're feeling ill, accept it, get appropriate cover for your class and go home.
- Leave a class on their own without telling anyone – even if you have to run out to the toilet! Always let another member of staff know.
- Go home without telling anyone – not only is it likely you will be disciplined, the school needs to know who is onsite for fire regulations.

26 Headaches and hangovers

It was your birthday yesterday, and last night you had a few too many down the pub. Today you have a full day to teach, an angry parent to telephone and a staff meeting to attend.

It seems that many of us, regardless of how old we get and how much of a professional we are, will always make the odd mistake, especially where alcohol is concerned. It's all very well saying 'never again!', but that hangover is going to stay with you all day, and 'pulling a sickie' just isn't an option.

Going to school with a hangover or having drunk a little too much at lunchtime doesn't just affect you. It also affects your class in the following ways:

1   Reduced teacher performance in the classroom
2   Poor teacher judgement
3   Reduced learning opportunities for your students
4   Increased potential for accidents
5   Poor time-keeping or motivation

 Be aware: it is worth remembering that teaching while under the influence of alcohol is a disciplinary offence. Actually receiving a disciplinary will usually depend on how much alcohol you have consumed, and how much it is seen to be affecting you. Most teachers can get away with the odd pint at lunchtime. Turning up to school drunk, however, is the sign of a poor or troubled teacher, and should *never* be done.

Getting rid of a hangover

Everyone has their own ideas on how to cure a hangover, from a greasy fry-up to 'hair of the dog' remedies. Of course, the best way to avoid a hangover is to avoid drinking too much the night before. However, if you've really overdone it and another day at school is looming, try the following tips:

- Drink plenty of water before you go to bed to help reduce the effects of dehydration, and keep drinking water throughout the day.

- Vitamin C is thought to be useful in curing hangovers. Try taking a Vitamin C tablet with your water before you go to sleep. Keep a glass of fruit juice by your bed in case you wake up in the night.
- If you really don't feel like eating in the morning, try fruit juice, yoghurt or warm water and honey. It is important to rehydrate yourself and boost your energy levels. A healthy but simple breakfast will do you good.
- Don't drink coffee or tea – these are diuretics that will dehydrate you even more.
- Simple analgesics (painkillers) can help with headaches, but for drug-free pain relief, try rubbing a little lavender oil on your temples.

 Remember: never drink on an empty stomach! Food slows down the absorption of alcohol. Before you start drinking, line your stomach with something solid, like bread, or a non-acidic drink like milk.

27 I'm sorry, I can't come in today

Everyone gets poorly sometimes, and working in schools exposes you to a lot of nasty bugs. Until your immune system strengthens itself (and it will!), you have to be prepared to spend up to the first term ill in one way or another.

> On my teaching practice, I worked out that I was ill in some way at least every other week. No sooner had I got rid of one cold, than another one hit me. I spent the first eight weeks with a totally blocked-up nose, so when I finally got better, the kids were asking me why my accent had changed. They had got so used to me sounding so nasal, they thought that was just what my voice was like!
>
> *Jane, Modern Foreign Languages teacher (25)*

It is important to decide just how ill you really are. Some teachers refuse to go to work even if they have a slight cold, their argument being that they do not want to spread it around. Other teachers would continue going to work even if both their legs had dropped off! As in all jobs, some people have stronger constitutions that others, but if you really do feel lousy, then don't feel guilty if you do need some time off. 'Pulling a sickie', however, because of an important football game, high street sale or simple laziness, is a very poor attitude to have.

 Be aware: never underestimate the knock-on effects one teacher being off sick can have on a school. When you are off ill, your usual classes need to be covered, often by other regular teaching staff. Your usual school duties need to be adhered to. Cover materials need to be found if you haven't had the foresight to leave any work, and your department will be running one man down. While you lounge around on your sofa at home, you can be sure that your work colleagues are less than ecstatic about your absence.

Things to do if you really are poorly

- Let your school know at the earliest possible opportunity by telephoning them yourself. Tell them what is wrong and when you think you will be back – be realistic!
- Leave instructions for your day's lessons so that your department doesn't need to panic and your classes keep on top of their work.
- Make sure you consider all your duties, including any meetings you may be due to attend, and ensure your colleagues know what to expect.
- Take advantage of the Internet and email if you have it – send any lesson plans and materials to your colleagues.
- If you have keys or other materials that need to be at the school, help as much as you can to get them on site.

 Remember: it is important you get better, and take the time off that you need, but don't encourage the possibility of earning a bad reputation by being 'ill' too often. You will only end up making things more stressful for yourself, because of having to chase up cover teachers and find out what you've missed while you were away.

Set a positive role model for your class: the more time you take off ill, the more time they will too. Schools do as much as they can to encourage full attendance, and that means teaching staff too!

28 Dealing with tiredness

Even when you've been teaching for years, being tired is something that can easily sneak up on you. Getting back into the swing of things after the school holidays can be particularly hard. After all those lovely long lie-ins and working at a steady pace, going back to 6 a.m. starts and a hectic work schedule can be really draining.

It's not surprising that you might feel tired when you consider how much work an average teacher does in a week, with many of us burning the midnight oil to get all our planning and preparation sorted for the week ahead. Add to that any family worries, financial stresses, and other unexpected disruptions, and there will almost definitely be times when exhaustion gets the better of you.

Work-related stress and exhaustion are real concerns in four out of five UK schools. Too much work and not enough relaxation can lead to impaired psychological and physical performance, resulting in a complete burnout if circumstances remain unchecked. Many teachers are actually ashamed to admit that they are feeling tired or stressed, as they think it is a sign of weakness. It is a sad fact that stress is now cited as the number one reason for leaving the teaching profession.

Dropping off in the middle of a lesson is a good clue to how tired you are, but you shouldn't be waiting until such an extreme example occurs! Listen to your body, your family and your colleagues. If people are commenting on how tired you're looking, don't take umbrage, question why they might be saying that. If you're finding it a real battle to get out of bed in the morning, take a good look at how many hours sleep you're getting and if you're really giving yourself time to wind down.

Top tips to avoid tiredness

- Avoid caffeine! This will only give you a temporary 'high' and will leave you feeling even more tired when the drug wears off.
- Drink plenty of water. Good practice is up to eight glasses a day, but simply drinking enough to keep yourself properly hydrated will stop you feeling sleepy.
- Having frequent, small meals will help combat tiredness after eating.
- Exercising regularly will encourage feel-good endorphin hormones and help you sleep better. Yoga is especially good at helping you beat tiredness.

- Get at least seven to eight hours uninterrupted sleep a night. Lavender pillows are very good for helping you to drop off.
- Set yourself boundaries on your work – don't try and burn the candle at both ends just to get things done. Focus on the quality of your work not the quantity.

Working while tired isn't just bad for your emotional and physical well-being, it might even mean you are putting your class at risk if you are not alert enough to spot potential problems in your class. This is especially true if you are a Physical Education or Technology teacher, where potentially dangerous equipment is being used.

 Be aware: always make sure you are the best you can be whenever you step into the classroom; you are responsible for the welfare of your students.

29 AWOL alarm clocks and traffic jams

Even the best teachers run late sometimes and, just like any other job, it is essential that you let people at the school know what is going on.

Alarm clocks do break, family catastrophes will happen early in the morning, and even the most carefully planned route to school can fall foul to a traffic jam.

 Remember: as soon as you know, or even suspect, you're going to be late, telephone someone at the school, particularly if you are a form tutor.

Dashing into the daily staffroom briefing five minutes late is permissible; arriving for registration ten minutes late isn't. Your duty of care stipulates that at certain times of the day you are expected to be taking care of particular classes. If you are not able to be there on time, there can be no telling what chaos might occur in your absence!

Similarly, if you suspect you are going to be more than a few minutes late, then cover lessons need to be arranged and supply or cover teachers organized. Keeping your colleagues informed is a must.

The top ten causes of lateness

It might seem like a teacher's life is ruled by the clock and timetables, and most people slip into the time-keeping routine very quickly. However, some things simply cannot be planned for:

1 Car troubles – flat tyres/batteries, etc.
2 Traffic jams, accidents and road works
3 Alarm clock disasters
4 Family member or pet being ill
5 Lost keys
6 Domestic appliance troubles
7 Mislaid marking/homework/lesson plans, etc.
8 Battles for the bathroom
9 Other family emergencies
10 Non-serious accidents, illnesses or mishaps

30 Chilling out and switching off

Although you may have chosen teaching as your career, this doesn't mean it has to become your whole life! Many teachers get so bogged down in the work they have to do, they forget about the people they were before they became teachers. Don't let this happen to you!

It is good to feel passionate about your job, and it's easy to slip into the trap of talking about it all the time (especially if things are a bit tough), but there really is more to life than just teaching. No, honestly, there is!

Do you really want to get to retirement age having spent your whole life surrounded by young people so much that you have almost forgotten how to interact with other adults? You might think this is rather far-fetched, but just think about all the typical 'school-marms' you have met. Some people teach for so long they treat *everyone* like one of their students!

 Remember: take time to switch off, and grab some time out from teaching every day. It is essential that you wind down and relax at the end of each teaching day, or you may end up trying to push yourself too far and stressing yourself unnecessarily.

Set yourself a particular time each evening when you take off your 'teacher hat' and become *you*. That means putting away the marking, planning and organizing and really switching off from the day's work. Never neglect your hobbies for the sake of your career. If possible, cultivate an interest in something that is completely removed from teaching, be it trainspotting, badminton or gardening.

For a completely teaching-free zone, try these tips:

- Find a place at home where you can do and keep all your teaching work – don't take it into a room where you relax, keep it separate so you can walk away and switch off from it.
- If you find that school work takes over your free time, allocate specific amounts of time to each area of your life. For example, spend no more than two hours each week night on school work, and keep your weekends completely teaching-free.

- If you must discuss your work, keep it to a minimum. Teachers have a terrible habit of talking about nothing but teaching! This is fine if everyone you know is a teacher, but will soon become boring for partners, family and friends if they're not part of the education profession.
- As much as you can, switch off from teaching as soon as you leave the school premises. Keep in mind that you are not just 'sir' or 'miss': you are a person as well.
- Put as much effort into your hobbies as you do into your work, and enjoy yourself!
- During the school holidays, make sure you keep at least two weeks for a real holiday, not just more planning and marking. Many teachers use the holidays to catch up, and so never really get a true holiday from their work. Go somewhere completely new and leave your school work behind!
- Have an active social life and wide network of friends. Don't just socialize with your work colleagues.

Although it is good to be passionate about something you enjoy, it can also be dangerous to let this passion consume you. If your entire life is spent focused on teaching, then perhaps something needs to change.

Work to live, don't live to work!

31 Stress, depression and taking time off

Sadly, one of the major causes of people leaving the teaching profession is stress-related illness. This is no surprise when you consider how stressful the job can be. Many teachers, particularly those who are new to teaching, often feel completely overwhelmed by the pressures of the job. Perhaps what is more worrying is that they come to accept that this is simply part of what teaching is all about, and can often end up exhausting themselves trying to meet the many demands.

While all jobs have a certain element of stress and challenge to them, when your job becomes a constant uphill struggle and it's beginning to make you miserable, then it is time to stop, take some time to chill out, and reassess what you really want out of your career.

Never be ashamed to admit that you are having problems or difficulties. It is much better to ask for help than try to struggle on. Stress is *not* a sign of weakness.

Stress can affect you physically, behaviourally, mentally and emotionally. If you are already exhibiting signs of excessive tiredness and fatigue, this is a sure sign that your health is being affected. Constant or repeated stress can even contribute to major illnesses such as heart disease, ulcers, diabetes and severe depression (stress and depression are frequently linked, because prolonged, negative stress can have a considerable impact on the body's serotonin level).

Major symptoms of stress include:

- Excessive tiredness or fatigue
- Sleep disorders such as insomnia
- Nervousness or irritability
- Substance abuse such as alcohol, nicotine or other stimulants
- Changes in appetite
- Headaches
- Nausea and digestive complaints
- Decrease in concentration and memory
- Depression

Stress, depression and anxiety should always be taken seriously. These are real illnesses and require proper, professional help and guidance. If a medical/professional considers you to be suffering from one of these illnesses, ensure that you listen.

Symptoms of depression include:

- Prolonged sadness or unexplained crying
- Significant changes in appetite and sleeping
- Persistent tiredness, fatigue and lethargy
- Severe mood swings or changes
- Loss of motivation or interest in former enthusiasms
- Unexplained physical symptoms – aches, pains, nausea, etc.
- Recurring thoughts of death or suicide

Many teachers believe that if they carry on and ignore the symptoms, things will miraculously resolve. If you broke your leg, you would not expect to be running a race after three weeks. The same logic applies to stress and depression. Make sure you take the time you need to get better.

1 Tell someone – a colleague, your Head of Department, a member of the management team. Do not feel like you have to suffer alone, or that you have failed in some way. Admitting you need some help is the first step to getting better.

2 Get professional medical advice and support. Many GPs are very used to teachers complaining of stress and will happily sign you off work for a couple of weeks. If that is what is recommended, take it. It is better to take a couple of weeks off than burn yourself into the ground and end up taking many months off.

3 Change your thinking – look at things in a positive way and learn from the experience. You might not even have realized you were doing so much until you stop.

4 Remember that you will beat it. Discovering that you have a breaking point simply means you are a human being – and every human being has different strengths and weaknesses. You do not have to be Superman to excel in your job, and it is just as important to enjoy your career as it is to be successful in it.

If you do take some time off, ensure things have changed when you return. Don't simply jump back into the same stressful routine you followed before your leave.

Teaching is a team profession, so make sure you are getting help and support from your department. Delegate and share tasks as much as you can, and don't feel like you have to do everything yourself.

Be aware: teacher stress is very common and, while it is good that the illness is recognized more by the medical profession, it has also become a bit too easy to use it as an excuse.

Faking a stress-related disorder just to get a couple of weeks off work is highly unprofessional, and is a good sign that it might be time for you to look for employment elsewhere!

32 Misery in the staffroom

Everybody has an 'off' day once in while, and even some of the best teachers have to have a little cry in the staffroom sometimes. It's not just female teachers either: I've seen even the toughest male reach for the tissues on occasion!

Whatever else is going on in your life, it doesn't necessarily stop as soon as you get through the school gates, regardless of how professional you are and how much you put it out of your mind. Alternatively, sometimes a low mood can be due to the stresses and pressures of your work, and you know nothing else will make you feel better than having a good sob.

For the experienced teacher, yet another teaching student sniffling into a handkerchief is a familiar sight. It is a common complaint among new or trainee teachers that sometimes the job gets to you in ways you don't expect. But don't be discouraged; letting it all out in the staffroom can be a good way of dealing with any stresses, and there is no shortage of other teachers who will try to cheer you up.

If ever you feel you are the only new teacher to feel completely and utterly disheartened by the job, be assured that you are not! It is not uncommon for all new teachers to go through periods of self-doubt, worry and stress. Adjusting to the sheer amount of work you are expected to do can make you feel very tired and worn out, and as a consequence you might find you end up feeling quite teary.

It's not just new or inexperienced staff that snivel in the staffroom, experienced teachers do it too: the difference is that they are often much better at hiding it! Crying is the body's way of dealing with emotion; don't deny yourself a cry if you really need one.

Remember:

- Crying in front of your class or indeed in front of any students is best avoided. You may well get plenty of sympathy from your surprised students, but your reputation may get tainted in the process!
- Having a bit of a cry in the staffroom or toilets isn't a bad thing – you're not the first and you certainly won't be the last to do so.
- Crying helps you to deal with and release any troublesome emotions, which is why you often feel much better after a good cry. However, if you are crying every day or for no real reason, seek help, as this can be a sign of stress and/or depression.

You As a Person, Not Just a Teacher

33 What not to wear

As a member of the education profession, it is essential to remember that you are a role model to your students, and as such you need to look the part. While low-cut tops might be the latest fashion, or you have a passion for neon green ties, it is important to remember that how you look will also influence how you are perceived.

Some items of clothing really shouldn't make it into the classroom. Although most of these are obvious, such as micro miniskirts, Bermuda shorts and offensive (or even football) t-shirts, some items such as tight-fitting trousers or very low-cut tops may also give your colleagues cause to complain.

As a general rule of thumb, if your students wear a uniform, then you should do too. This doesn't mean you have to turn up in the official school colours every day, but you should be taking into serious consideration the messages you may be giving out through your choice of dress.

> I have always worn a lot of black, mainly because it is a nice, simple colour, and means I don't have to worry too much about finding things that match. I don't really bother about fashion too much, and I've had a ponytail since I was 17.
>
> I never really considered what kind of image I was giving out; until I found out that the students had nicknamed me 'Dracula'!
>
> *Gareth, ICT teacher (26)*

Tips on what to wear

- Different types of schools may have different expectations on how you are supposed to dress. If you are unsure, always dress up rather than down.
- Ensure your clothes are appropriate to the subject you teach – e.g. wearing a suit every day when you teach Physical Education is very impractical.
- Consider health and safety regulations in accordance with your dress – long hair and trailing sleeves can get caught in machines.
- Be smart but be comfortable – high heels may give you added height, but they will also give you blisters if you are on your feet all day.

- Keep hairstyles and make-up neat, simple and toned down. Dyed green hair or livid lipsticks are not appropriate for the classroom! (Unless they are for a charity event, of course.)
- Don't be afraid to express your individuality in other ways – through interesting jewellery, funky-coloured socks or crazy ties. Looking smart doesn't mean you have to be borings and students are always fascinated by teachers with quirks.
- Non-uniform days can be a bit of a wardrobe nightmare. If you are in any doubt, a pair of jeans and a plain coloured top or shirt will usually be okay.
- Clothing that is too tight, too revealing or simply too 'trendy' for the classroom should be avoided at all costs.
Ladies: don't forget how bending and stretching can unintentionally reveal any areas you would prefer left covered.
- Tattoos and body piercing are best covered up. Different schools will have varying policies on these. Although they have no bearing on your actual teaching ability, wherever possible keep these discreet or hidden.

34 Mind your language

Most teachers have a 'teacher voice', which is a bit like having a telephone voice. The way teachers speak and the kinds of things they say are very particular to the occupation. There is a certain level of expectation surrounding a teacher's vocabulary.

All teachers know that swearing in the classroom or at students is unprofessional and completely unacceptable. But what about other things you say that get misinterpreted?

Unintentional innuendoes are some of the worse culprits. Most of the time you won't even be aware what you've said until you hear the entire class tittering away. Telling a student to 'just get it out' (his pen), or 'spit it out or swallow it' (a sweet), is guaranteed to have every class member over the age of 13 giggling in glee. Don't forget schoolyard colloquialisms either: even the innocent pencil eraser, known to some as a 'rubber', can be considered rude since someone decided it shares its name with a form of contraceptive!

Your *sotto voce* – the things you mutter to yourself under your breath – can be a pitfall too. Although you might not mean your mutterings to be heard, sometimes they will be, and it is even worse if they are *mis*heard.

> During my teaching practice I was writing away on the whiteboard when I realized I needed to check a spelling of a difficult word. I was muttering away to myself anyway, and as I wandered over to my notes on my desk I said, under my breath, 'Actually. . .'. Unfortunately, what the observing teacher heard was, 'Oh, shit. . .', and marked it down on my observation sheet! I made a point of not mumbling anything to myself after that!
>
> *Paula, History teacher (27)*

Sometimes your temper makes you say things you later regret. Even the most calm and reasonable of teachers has been known to utter the odd expletive or questionable phrase when particularly riled.

 Remember: the old, yet very effective idea of 'counting to ten before you speak' to avoid any potential blunders.

Train yourself to respond instinctively with non-offensive phrases when bad or annoying things happen, such as 'drat', 'oh dear', 'fiddle-sticks' and 'crumbs'. They might sound terribly old fashioned, but they are much better than the more common (and not so pleasant) alternatives!

If you do accidentally swear in front of your students – and it does happen – it is often best to just pretend you didn't, and gloss over it! In most cases, your students will not be bothered by it at all, and if they do pick up on it, they will more than likely just find it amusing. As long as you don't make a habit of it, and never, ever purposefully swear at a child, the odd blooper is permissible.

 Be aware: in the rare event that you seriously lose your temper and use any form of taboo language directly at a student, be sure to document it in an incident report afterwards. Include exactly what you said, and tell your department head or senior management straight away. Again, in most cases it is unlikely that you will suffer any serious repercussions, but it is important that you are seen to have recognized your mistake and that you are prepared to accept responsibility for it.

35 Getting the bus to school

Sometimes you have no choice but to take the bus to school. This may be because your car has broken down, is getting its MOT, or you simply haven't passed your driving test yet.

For many teachers, this is an experience akin to walking across hot coals. This is where you will get to see students for what they really are – outside of school in a public environment.

Be aware that the students, and you, are representing your school to the general public: but what most people don't consider is how far your authority actually goes. If a student is messing about on the bus, don't be surprised if other bus users expect *you* to sort it out!

> I frequently had to get the bus to school before I passed my driving test. On the route, there were three different schools, and three different sets of students. A group of lads from a school I didn't work at started throwing paper all over the bus. An old man tapped me on the shoulder and asked me, very indignantly, 'Well, are you going to tell them off or what?' I apologized and told him that I was sorry but I did not know or teach those particular students. His reply was, 'But you're a teacher aren't you? Surely you can do *something* about them!' I was so embarrassed to find that everyone on the bus was staring at me, including the students, and I didn't have a clue what to say or do!
>
> *Michael, Geography teacher (24)*

Some schools fully support public transport for school children by stationing a member of school staff on all journeys, who can act in the event of any disagreeable behaviour. However, unless you have been requested to do this by your employer, do not feel you are under any obligation to step into your 'teacher role' unless you really want to. On any form of public transport that is carrying passengers under the age of 16, the bus driver is considered to be the responsible adult in the event of any difficult or dangerous situation.

 Be aware: official regulations may differ depending on your local council or public transport provider.

- A bus driver has the legal authority to remove any passenger over the age of 16, excluding any pupils being taken to and from school, whose behaviour is causing a danger or nuisance to other passengers.
- School age children en route to or from school will not be removed from the vehicle, but if their behaviour is causing concern, or the safety of the child or other passengers is under question, then the driver may pull over and notify the police.
- In the interest of safety and protection of other passengers, the driver may refuse to carry an intending passenger if:
  - they are considered to be under the influence of alcohol or drugs
  - they are being violent or threatening to other passengers or to the driver
  - they are accompanied by a dog which is considered to be potentially dangerous.

36 A life outside of teaching

Having a social life outside of teaching might seem like a dream to some teachers, particularly those who are new to the profession, but it *is* possible.

In the initial stages of training, the NQT year, and indeed, anything up to the third year of teaching, it can seem like your entire life is taken up with teaching. For many it is also a very 'addictive' career, where they actually enjoy putting their hearts and souls into their profession.

It is certainly no bad thing to be passionate about your career, and have a positive drive and a desire to succeed: but it is also essential to maintain some balance between work and home life. As I have already said, if you don't make time for other interests outside of teaching, there is a danger that you can end up forgetting what kind of person you were before you taught.

Keeping your social and working life separate can seem impossible at first, but you must set yourself a clear dividing line and absolutely refuse to cross it at any cost! Whatever it is that is driving you – teaching may be your dream job, or you are simply desperate to pass your induction with flying colours – you must make time to look after yourself.

- Don't let teaching absorb you or your free time – set yourself clear limits.
- Give yourself realistic deadlines for school and housework – make sure you also have free time to relax.
- Don't neglect your family and friends – make time for outside interests and socializing.
- Consider alternative therapies to help manage stress, such as aromatherapy, massage, yoga or meditation, or some form of sport.
- Although it might be tempting to use the holidays to catch up on work, give yourself a break too. You deserve it.
- Eat sensibly and healthily and get plenty of sleep – don't try to burn the candle at both ends just to get more work done.
- You are not Superman or Superwoman: accept your limitations as a human being and don't take on more work than you can realistically handle.
- If you find yourself turning down social events because you are 'too busy', then you are not managing your time effectively. Your career may be important, but so are you!

Remember: if you found out that you only had one year left to live, would you still think your career was worth sacrificing your free time and social life for? Remind yourself why you wanted to become a teacher but don't let your job take over your life.

37 Bringing up Baby – Mixing 'Mummy' with 'Miss'

Teachers are paid to educate and look after other people's children. However, it is very important not to forget about your own, or the rest of your family.

Spouses and partners can often feel pushed out, especially if they don't really understand the expectations of the teaching profession. During particularly busy periods at school, it can be hard to set aside some real quality time for you and your family. I know of many teachers who say that a lot of arguments at home begin because their partner thinks they are putting the school before their family.

Whether you are single, married or in a relationship, never forget what is the most important thing in your life: your career or your happiness?

For female teachers who are expecting a baby, the pressures of teaching can be very demanding. In the first trimester you are likely to be feeling very tired, nauseous and quite hormonal, and a heavy teaching load will not help. It is important to get as much sleep as you need: if necessary, delegate to colleagues and ask them to help you with your marking and preparation. There is no reason at all that teaching should affect a pregnancy or vice versa, but as in all areas of employment a thorough risk assessment must be done, preferably at the earliest opportunity.

The kinds of risk areas assessed will include:

- Any continuous standing or sitting?
- Any excess travelling?
- Any exposure to harmful chemicals or cigarette smoke?
- Any possible work-related violence or excessive stress?
- Any heavy lifting or manual handling?

It is important to consider how the risks apply to specific individuals and circumstances.

Current UK law states that you must notify your employer in writing that you are pregnant, and intend to take maternity leave, no later than the end of the fifteenth week before your child is due. Most women are happy enough to inform their employer well before this date. Ordinary maternity leave is for 26 weeks, but you may be entitled to take up to a year off if you need to. Bear in mind that you may be requested to provide work to cover your absence for this period.

For teachers with young children, there may be additional pressures to find adequate childcare. While teaching hours are considered to be much more flexible than many other jobs, you will still be required to be on site on average between 8:30 a.m. and 4 p.m. each day, and you will need to find a childcare provider that can accommodate your needs.

Some teachers are happy to enrol their older children at the school in which they work, which can be both a blessing and curse for both of you! It is essential that your child understands that while you are at work he or she must treat you as they would any other teacher, and you must treat them like all of your other students.

Teaching is one of the few jobs that will allow you to have the same days off and holidays as your children, and even if you bring work home with you, it is likely that you will be arriving home around the same time as your kids. Your children may also benefit from your knowledge of your subject, and might even find an interest in teaching themselves. Even if it is unintentional, you will be helping to encourage and expand your children's education.

38 Bumping into students outside of school

It would be naïve to think that you will only ever see your students inside school. Often you see them in town on a Saturday afternoon. Sometimes you see them at the cinema and, if you teach at post-16 level, sometimes you even go to the same pubs and clubs!

One of the strange mysteries of life is why students find the idea of teachers having a life outside of school so incredibly fascinating. Any interesting snippets of gossip about what you do at the weekend or what your partner looks like will always be lapped up eagerly. This explains why, if you do see your students outside of school, you can guarantee that:

- they will almost certainly try to stop you and engage in some small talk with you
- you will get grilled about your antics once you get back to the school.

 Remember: to avoid any gossip, always be as honest as you can about your life away from school, but don't feel like you have to give away too much information. It is not advisable to tell students any specific details that they do not need to know, such as where you live, which clubs or shops you frequent, or information about your family.

If you do bump into students outside of school, take time to be friendly and say hello, but make it obvious that you are also doing things in your own time, in order to discourage students 'hanging on'. While your employer may desire you to be a positive role model and ambassador for the school at all times, this is not always possible – you are entitled to have a life outside school after all!

However, regardless of how embarrassing or awkward any chance meetings may be, stay positive and in control and, if necessary, slip briefly into your 'teacher mode' until you can make your escape!

39 I know where you live

As a teacher you will be given personal information about your classes, including their home address and telephone numbers. It is important that you know where your students live, so that they and their families can be contacted if necessary. However, if your place of work is just down the road from your house, it is inevitable that some students will find out where *you* live.

There is no need to start searching the estate agent ads just yet, as this doesn't have to be a problem. Once you learn to ignore the comments such as 'You live on the same street as me, Miss' and 'Your garden's a right mess, Sir!', living near to your students can also bring a sense of community into your life.

There are some occasions when, if a student knows where you live, it can be a very bad thing. Every so often you may come across a student who holds a grudge against you – perhaps he did not agree with your detention decision, or she believed she should have got a higher mark on her essay – and a small handful of these types of students often feel that revenge is the way forward.

 Be aware: never let anyone, particularly one of your students, intimidate you at home. You have the right to contact the police straight away if you are at all concerned about any student's behaviour around your home. If you know the student, you may be tempted to deal with the issue at school, but this can get difficult when it is not a school-based incident. Engage the support of your peers and management team and ensure proper action is taken to prevent any further incidents.

When I first started teaching, I got a job with the school ten minutes away from my house. The trouble is, when the students find out where you live, they seem to think it's perfectly fine to come knocking on your door asking for help with their homework, or even just for a chat!

I now work at a school over eight miles away. It requires more travelling but at least once I'm home I can leave my classes behind!

Josephine, Humanities teacher (36)

40 If I don't laugh, I'll cry

Keeping your sense of humour can be hard if you've had a bad day. Getting angry or upset is far easier to do than laughing it off and not letting things get to you, but it is not the most productive way of dealing with problems.

A grumpy teacher is invariably not going to perform as well as a happy teacher. The obvious reasons for this are a noticeable lack of patience, a more abrupt and inaccessible manner and a tendency to maintain distance rather than engage with the students.

 Remember: the best piece of advice I can give any teacher is: *never take anything too personally.*

Even if you have had an awful morning and everything seems to have gone wrong, it is imperative to have the ability to switch off, move on and not let things have a knock-on effect on your work. Every day is a new day, and you should be prepared to face it with a clean slate. This means you can give yourself the chance to wind down and process any problems, and if necessary learn from them.

Although it might not be possible always to come into work with a smile on your face, it is helpful to try! Even periods of high stress can be combated with a sunny outlook. The more you worry, the worse any little niggles will seem! If you have a positive attitude and a good sense of humour, you will find things to make you laugh every day when you work in a school.

Laughter is good for you! It can:

- Reduce the levels of chronic stress in your body.
- Enhance your lifespan.
- Help your circulation.
- Boost your immune system function.
- Protect your nervous system.
- Give your endocrine system a break.
- Keep you sane!

And it's free!

(See the movie *Patch Adams* (1998) for further clarification.)

41 Your reputation with students

You might be firm but fair, you might be fun and cheerful, or perhaps you're a very stern teacher indeed, but how do you get the reputation you want with your students, and more importantly, how do you keep it?

From your very first meeting with the students you teach, they will be forming opinions about you from first impressions, just as you will about them. In addition to how you act as a teacher, even your clothes, accent and haircut will be projecting aspects of your personality. It is a good idea to use these early sessions to establish ground rules and expectations, as well as using it as time to get to know your class.

Due to the nature of the job your reputation will precede you – even if you don't want it to.

Top tips for good practice

- There is little point putting on an act for your students – engage your 'teacher mode', but be yourself as well.
- Start the year as you want it to continue. There is no point coming across in your initial meetings as fun and relaxed, only to become harsh and inapproachable within a couple of weeks.
- Always take an interest in your class and engage with them, but never make the mistake of trying to be their 'friend'. Getting too close to a student will only cause complications in the long run, and is not considered good, professional practice.
- A good teacher takes interest in their students in a wide variety of situations. Take time to talk to them at break and lunch times and after school, and really get to know them as people, rather than just individuals to be taught.

42 Embarrassing incidents

Teachers are humans too, but sometimes they don't want their students to know that! Perhaps you tucked your skirt into your pants, left your flies undone or that curry last night has left you feeling a bit 'windy'.

There seems to be a very prevalent idea among teachers – especially those who have taught for a long time – that they should be some sort of mystical, authoritarian being. It is not considered good to let the students see their human side.

In reality, this is not only impractical, but also often quite impossible. Not to mention that it gives students an unrealistic impression of what teachers are like.

 Remember: embarrassing incidents will and do happen to teachers at some point or another, and the best way to deal with them is to keep a good sense of humour.

You will be far more likely to get away with something silly or embarrassing if you laugh it off, rather than getting flustered or wound up about it. Although you may wish the ground would open and swallow you, and you may have to put up with a few humorous names or stories being told about you, it's not the end of the world.

Top ten embarrassing things that can happen in the classroom

1 Unexpected bodily functions: belching, flatulence, rumbling stomach, etc.
2 Clothing problems: rips, stains, see-through materials, tops/skirts that 'ride up', misbehaving zippers/buttons, etc.
3 Food stuck between the teeth
4 Smuts and mucky marks – especially on the face
5 Uncomfortable or visible underwear
6 Slips, trips, dropping and walking into things
7 Freudian slips and innuendoes
8 Getting names mixed up, especially when disciplining a student
9 Drawings/diagrams that look unintentionally rude
10 Spelling words wrong on the board

43 Strange things kids say (and write)

One of the most amusing, and often perplexing, sides to teaching is the strange things your students may say or write, either in the classroom, or their homework. Even when you think you have heard it all, there will still be some little darling who brightens up your day with a gem of 'wisdom'.

Often their blunders are down to misunderstanding a topic, mishearing a new word, or mistakenly attempting to bring a new word or idea into their vocabulary.

If a student unintentionally uses an inappropriate verbal word or phrase, try to correct him or her gently, and avoid any possible embarrassment in front of peers. Children are always very quick to pick up on another's mistakes and use them against them. Always be tactful and honest, and never laugh openly at a student's mistake – whatever their age.

Some children like to try out new words in class, especially rude or offensive ones! Rather than being angry or embarrassed, tell the student that particular word is unacceptable and is not to be used. Be prepared for students asking 'why?', but don't feel like you have to embellish any further than you want to. If a student uses a word in the incorrect context or as an insult, explain why this is not acceptable but show how the word can be used correctly.

Once students discover swearing, you can be sure they will be eager to try it out. Swearing can make children feel grown up or independent, or they may do it to fit in with their peers. Always discourage any form of swearing: however, try to explain that swearing is not necessarily *bad*, but that it gives others a negative impression of you and there are far better ways to communicate your emotions.

There may be some occasions when you have no idea what the student is trying to say. This is normal and is a usual part of amusing staffroom anecdotes!

 Remember: every teacher will be able to tell you a story about the weirdest things they have heard students say, some being ruder or more risqué than others. Recounting an amusing classroom tale can also be an excellent staffroom icebreaker.

A large percentage of the examples I could give here would be far too rude to print! The following are some of the more tame ones:

God is said to be impotent which means he is all powerful.

Octopuses have eight long testicles with sticky bits on the end.

Squirrels like hiding their nuts in the winter, because other animals try to steel them.

James had flu and Paul wasn't alloyed to go and see him because his Mum was scared he might catsh*it.

Pupil to teacher: 'I can't believe you only gave me an 'F' for my essay. My Mum spent ages on that!'

Teacher: 'What kinds of stories might you find in a fiction book?'
Pupil: 'Harry Potter!'

Pupil: 'Miss, can I have a pen?'
Teacher: 'What's the magic word?'
Pupil: 'Abracadabra?'

One pupil who continually did not hand in his homework, and had done multiple detentions, was in trouble again for failing to hand in a two-week project. He handed me some print-outs off the Internet and told me he had spent four weeks doing them and that they were all his own work. What he failed to notice is that he had the website address, date and time printed on the bottom, so I knew he was lying as it showed he had printed them out the night before!

Melanie, History teacher (29)

44 It's all about sex, baby – Taboo subjects

The National Curriculum dictates guidelines for teaching Personal, Social and Health Education (PSHE) and Citizenship in partnership with other Curriculum subjects. This ensures pupils are given some essential information on subjects such as drug, tobacco and alcohol use, and sexual and relationship education. Form tutors and teachers with no specialist experience in the subjects teach most PSHE sessions. This means that if you have a form class allocated to you, you may well be responsible for teaching these issues to your class.

PSHE lessons should include practical discussions on everyday issues, to encourage understanding of 'taboo' subjects. Sex, contraception, abortion, bullying, mental health and family issues are all a part of preparing students for life outside of education, and should be taught sensitively and honestly.

 Remember: many teachers feel embarrassed about teaching these kinds of subjects to young people, or think that this should be a parental responsibility. It is important to remember that ignorance frequently leads to misunderstanding.

Young people today are allegedly exposed to far more potentially disturbing material than previous generations, and as a consequence are likely to have a reasonable understanding of these subjects already. Don't be surprised if your class seems to know far more about sex than you do! In addition, these young people are just beginning to form their own opinions on these issues. It is much better to present them with the information they can use to make their minds up, rather than trying to influence their decisions.

Helpful tips for teaching PSHE topics

- Don't be embarrassed, regardless of the subject matter – remember, you are the teacher and you are in control.
- Children genuinely want to know all the facts. Answer their questions honestly and openly.
- Make discussions open and frank, but don't stray into too personal areas. Remember that some students feel very awkward when talking about how they feel.

- Be sensitive to students' upbringing, life experiences and religion: be aware that some areas may make students feel uncomfortable and upset. Areas such as bereavement, abortion or abuse can be particularly tricky.
- Use the QCA frameworks to give you a solid understanding of what you should be teaching.
- Be prepared to answer students' questions. If the subject is of a delicate nature, ask students to write their questions down and place them in a box. This gives you more control over, and preparation time to deal with, potentially awkward queries.
- Have a good sense of humour – making difficult subjects light-hearted can be hard work, but will help you and your students relax.

45 Teaching is not a popularity contest

Everyone wants to be liked, and teachers are no exception. If you're new to the job, or new to the school, it can be a daunting task trying to earn the acceptance of your new students.

 Remember: your job is to teach the students, not to try and gain new friends.

No matter how cool, hip and 'with it' you might think you are, you can be sure that your students strongly disagree! Never, ever try to use popular or trendy words or phrases seriously. Adding words such as 'bling', 'dude', or 'bangin', to your vocabulary will only make you look outdated and desperate. However young you are or feel, you are not 'one of the kids' and it is a real mistake to try to be!

It is clear that a popular, approachable and well-liked teacher is also a good one, and is likely to have much better controlled classes. It isn't that hard to maintain a professional relationship with your students, while at the same time being open and friendly, by simply taking a genuine interest in each child.

 Be aware: young people can spot insincerities instantly, and are unlikely to put up with being patronized any more than an adult would, so never just *pretend* to be interested!

Regardless of how well-liked you might be by 99 per cent of your students, there will always be the 1 per cent that simply doesn't get on with you. It is impossible to get on with everyone! Don't take it to heart, and also don't try to force the relationship to improve – you will only end up alienating that particular student even more. If eventually they decide you're not that bad after all, they will come to you and make it known.

The most important thing to remember is to be friendly, open and honest with your classes, and the odd joke or silly story doesn't hurt either. A truly likeable teacher will find that popularity comes to them; they do not need to strive for it.

Top tips for being a successful teacher

1 Have a genuine sense of humour and the ability to laugh at yourself.
2 Have a positive and proactive attitude.
3 Be firm but fair and keep rules and guidelines consistent.
4 Have high expectations of all your students, and communicate this to them regularly.
5 Be rational and non-judgemental: treat all your students equally.
6 Have a flexible attitude and be ready to adapt to any situation.

46 A Valentine from Tommy Smith

My first crush, at the age of 14, was on my Technology teacher. I thought he was gorgeous and Technology became my favourite subject for a while. I forgot all about this until years later when I became a teacher myself and suddenly realized that one particular Year 9 boy was being incredibly attentive in my classes!

A student crush doesn't have to be a problem, in fact, it can be quite sweet and flattering in some cases, but it goes without saying that it is not something to be encouraged! If it does become uncomfortable, or you feel that the student's behaviour has become inappropriate, it is essential to tackle the issue directly. Remind the student that you are the teacher and that there are clear boundaries that will never be crossed. Try not to get into situations where you may be left on your own with the student, and avoid any physical contact with him or her. If you are really worried, it is a good idea to tell a colleague about the crush, in case it becomes a bigger problem.

Most student crushes are harmless and the student will grow out of them in time. Remember that once they reach a certain age, these young bodies are being surged with unfamiliar hormones and feelings that they might not be sure how to deal with just yet.

Student crushes are often more to do with the teacher's passion for their subject and authoritative personality than their physical attributes. Your confidence and dominance in the classroom can actually make you desirable!

 Be aware: *never, ever* take advantage of this, and *never* encourage crushes. Your position dictates that you act as a professional role model for young people. Encouraging interests or activities of a sexual nature in school-age children is a direct contravention of your duty of care, and is illegal.

Even teachers of post-16 students should be aware that any romantic involvement with their students might mean their contract is terminated and their teaching record tainted.

What to do when a student has a crush on you

- Don't overreact, but make it obvious that these feelings are not reciprocated.

- Treat the student exactly the same as everyone else. Even if you feel awkward about the situation, do not ignore or embarrass the student, or make them feel bad in any way.
- Do not accept gifts or trinkets, regardless of how innocent they may seem – this may only encourage the student.
- Avoid one-to-one and physical contact with the student wherever possible.
- Discuss the situation with your colleagues if you feel you need to.
- If the student tries to contact you at home or out of school hours, be very clear that this is not acceptable and will not be tolerated.

Troublesome Times

47 When the pupils hate you

Sometimes, no matter how hard you try, your class just doesn't like you. Maybe it's because of a personality clash, or perhaps you simply got off to a bad start at the beginning of term. 'You can't win them all', as the saying goes – but unfortunately, you do still have to teach them.

 Be aware: before you resign yourself to a year of hell with this class, take a moment to try and determine where the problem might lie. Is it the whole class or just a few individuals? Is it because of their general behaviour, or are you being too harsh or unapproachable with them? Be prepared to accept that it might well be *you* who has the problem, and it is *your* attitude that might need to change.

Different types of students respond to different types of teachers and teaching styles. One of the main reasons why a teacher and class don't get on is the teaching style used. Always consider the ability range and subject material, and tailor your style accordingly. If you feel confident enough, you can even ask your students how they think lessons could be improved. Although you might end up with a lot of silly answers, there might also be some hidden gems that can enlighten you as to how to make valuable changes.

Don't forget, there will be occasions when you really don't get on with certain students. This doesn't mean you have failed in any way; it can simply just be a clash of personalities, and the best you can really hope for is civility. Don't *try* to make a student like you by being overly friendly or by showing undue favouritism; it is more likely that your good intentions will merely backfire on you.

 Remember: a happy teacher equals a happy class.

To ensure you gain, and keep, a good relationship with your students, always treat them in the way you would want to be treated yourself. If you give respect you will gain respect, and this is a fundamental foundation for a pleasant and productive working environment.

48 Dealing with 'problem' students

A 'problem' student isn't just one who behaves poorly. There is a whole range of things that can make a student troublesome to a teacher, from refusing to do as they are told, to having a particular special educational need.

Although teachers are expected to be able to deal with anything that is thrown at them, there is no shame in admitting that you find some areas particularly difficult.

> A student in my class was diagnosed with mild Tourette's Syndrome. I knew what this was and what it meant, but when he had an outburst in my lessons I found it very hard to cope with. There was a part of me that just wanted to shout at him and tell him to be quiet, even though I knew it wasn't his fault, and he wasn't doing it on purpose. I felt really guilty for feeling angry with him and I eventually talked to my Head of Department about it. She gave me some excellent resources and teaching tips on how to improve things.
>
> *Kath, English teacher (30)*

Always look at the 'problem' rationally and logically. Try to think of practical ways you might tackle the issue and alleviate the problem. Discuss your concerns with your colleagues, and if possible do some research into the problem. There are lots of helpful books and websites available which deal with specific educational issues.

 Remember: your job would be boring if you were not challenged in some way. You may find that once you stop worrying and pigeonholing certain individuals as a 'problem' they cease to be one.

49 Teenage angst (and how to deal with it)

Periods, spots, hormones and puberty – no wonder some teenagers can seem so angry all the time! Teenage angst – the term given to describe a time of emotional strife during the adolescent years – is a minefield for the students and the teachers alike, and is often the time when behaviour problems become more noticeable or difficult to deal with.

Not all teenagers succumb to periods of angst; many go through their adolescent years without any problems and enter young adulthood calmly and confidently. However, others find the process of growing up frustrating and difficult, and as a result will express this through anger or moodiness. Often this is simply due to them wanting to grow up too fast, or that they are finding it difficult to affirm themselves as individuals.

Much of their frustration often arises from being unable to express him or herself as they want to – perhaps they don't understand what is happening to them or are scared by the physical and emotional changes their bodies are going through. Some are even reluctant to let go of childhood and do not want to grow up. Whatever the reason, and however insignificant the problem may seem to you, it has a real impact on the student and should be treated seriously and sympathetically.

Dealing with teenage angst requires a lot of patience and understanding. Teenage temper tantrums and mood swings can be unpredictable, and it is best to use a gentle approach. Reassure the student that you are there to listen if they want to talk, and do not pass judgement on them. Give them opportunities to explore and express their feelings, and listen rather than advise. Try not to indulge the student too much, as inevitably some will use their 'problems' to excuse laziness or poor behaviour.

 Be alert: look out for any worrying signs that may indicate more serious problems. Problems such as adolescent depression can be difficult to spot, as teenagers frequently exhibit mood swings, negativity, sulkiness, antisocial behaviour, and withdrawal, simply as a normal part of them growing up!

A sudden decline in performance, major changes in mood or personality, or periods of illness or truancy may be signs that there is a deeper problem that needs investigating. Always inform your colleagues if you suspect this to be the case. Don't try to deal with it on your own.

Teenage depression is estimated to affect 5 per cent of adolescents at any point in time. It should be treated as seriously as adult depression: although the causes may be different, the symptoms and effects are the same. As the number of incidents of teenage depression documented increases, so too does the teen suicide rate. It is estimated that up to 90 per cent of teen suicides had suffered from some form of mental illness, including depression.

50 Calm down, cool off

There is a certain type of teacher who, when their temper gets the better of them, everyone else can hear from down the other end of the corridor!

Sometimes, having a reputation for being fierce isn't necessarily a bad thing, but if you find you are resorting to shouting on a regular basis, it is time to take a good look at your teaching and behaviour management techniques.

In an ideal world, teachers would never have to shout. A really good teacher very rarely does. Gaining and maintaining the command of the class does not mean you have to raise your voice. A firm, authoritative tone should be enough to establish who is the boss.

There will be days when things get on top of you and your blood starts to boil. Sometimes having a good shout can even be quite cathartic! However, shouting should be the very last resort. If you tackle every problem by raising your voice, you will soon find that you have shouted so much that it has no impact any more. Your students will switch off and stop listening to you.

How to avoid becoming known as a 'shouty' teacher

- Always strive to keep calm and be professional at all times.
- Always ensure you are in control of the situation. Count to ten before you react and keep your voice at a normal level.
- You should never need to shout just to get a class's attention: use visual signals if necessary and always wait for silence before you begin to speak.
- Remember: the quieter you speak, the more your class will have to pay attention to hear you.
- Tactically ignore unwanted behaviour where possible – don't make mountains out of molehills.
- Deal with problems firmly but fairly – take time to explain why something is unacceptable and ensure the class understands.

51 The good, the bad and the ugly (or, the 'do's and 'don't's of behaviour management)

Good behaviour management doesn't have to be daunting or difficult. Whatever happens, always make sure you stay in control, both of yourself and the situation. If you deal with poor behaviour quickly and efficiently, you will reduce the chances of it getting out of hand and escalating. Before you deal with *any* form of unwanted behaviour, make sure you give yourself the time to address the issue calmly. Count to ten if you need to and make sure you don't exhibit signs of poor behaviour of your own!

The 'do's of behaviour management

- Keep calm and be professional.
- Stay in control of the situation. Take your time to react accordingly to the problem.
- Encourage the student to take responsibility for their behaviour and give them the chance to change it.
- Make it clear that it is the behaviour that you are unhappy with, not the student personally.
- Set punishments that are firm but fair. Be consistent when explaining rules and expectations.
- Put poor behaviour into perspective: don't make mountains out of molehills.
- Ensure you know, and adhere to, school policies regarding discipline procedures.

The 'don't's of behaviour management

- Deal with a student when you are angry. Always give yourself the time to calm down and react rationally.
- Physically reprimand students: any form of hitting, pushing, grabbing, etc. is unacceptable.
- Invade a student's personal space – shouting in a student's face or being too close to them will make them feel threatened and they may react impulsively or violently.

- Attempt to humiliate the student, use sarcasm or pass personal judgements on them as an individual – focus only on the behaviour and what has happened, not on the student as a person.
- Give unrealistic or unfair punishments.
- Harbour grudges against students. Deal with and move on from the incident.
- Punish the whole class for one student's misbehaviour.

52 Behaviour management myths

There are lots of ways of approaching poor behaviour, many of which often depending on what kind of teacher you are. Some older teachers still believe in the 'old ways', back in the days when throwing a piece of chalk at a student to wake them up wasn't going to result in them taking out a lawsuit against you!

As times (and the curriculum) have changed, so too have behaviour management strategies. However, there are still a few stubborn myths that persist in classrooms across the country.

Myth 1 *Making the whole class stay behind when only one or two students have misbehaved will shame those individuals, and ensure they don't repeat their poor behaviour in the future.*

While allowing their peers to pass judgement might seem like an effective behaviour management strategy, in reality you are punishing the other students for something they haven't done. This will simply make the whole class resent you, and you will be tagged as an 'unfair' teacher.

Myth 2 *Removing an individual from the classroom means they have time to contemplate their actions and I can get on with my lesson.*

This is true, but also means you are denying that individual their right to education. Some students will misbehave with the whole aim of getting sent out because they simply do not like your subject! If you find you are sending the same student out of your room time and time again, then you need to take a good look at all the factors involved. Removing a student from your classroom is very 'lazy' behaviour management and shows that instead of being willing to deal with the problem, you would rather just get rid of it.

Myth 3 *If a student misbehaves they should be made to work on their own for the rest of the lesson.*

The act of singling out the individual and getting him or her to move around your class means you spend too much time giving the student negative attention, thus disrupting your lesson even more. Forcing a child to work on his or her own is also a form of exclusion within the classroom. Every child should be given the chance to work and interact with peers.

Myth 4 *Making a student stand in the corner of the room, or telling them off in front of the class will make an example of them and ensure they think twice about misbehaving again.*

Humiliating a child *is never* an acceptable form of behaviour management. Even if you think the child is 'tough' enough to cope with being judged in front of his or her peers, you may be surprised at how damaging this can be in the long term. 'Making an example' of a student only draws attention to their poor behaviour, and sends out negative messages. It is far better to draw attention to good behaviour and praise rather than admonish students in front of their classmates.

Myth 5 *Sitting students in boy-girl formation and making the class work in silence will ensure a calm and controlled class.*

This is a great idea in theory, but is hard to enforce in practice. Depending on the age range of the students, you may even find that this arrangement sparks off some budding romances! Silent classes can also be quite depressing, and allowing some quiet chatter will improve the learning atmosphere.

Myth 6 *Shouting is the best way of showing how angry you are and will ensure your students take you seriously.*

Shouting at a class is usually a sign that you have lost control. A good teacher will never need to shout and will find that talking in a calm, quiet voice gets far more results that merely bellowing at the students. I prefer the 'walk softly, carry a big stick' approach. If you establish a reputation that shows you won't tolerate certain kinds of behaviour, you should never need to resort to shouting.

Myth 7 *Detention is the most effective form of punishment a teacher can give.*

This depends on the student. For some, detention has become a daily occurrence and has lost all impact, while for others, gaining a detention is a mortifying experience. Take every factor into consideration before handing out punishments, in order to ensure that they are effective. It can be far too easy to hand out detentions for every little misdemeanour. Consider other punishments such as litter duty, working in the headmaster's office or removing computer privileges, as these can have more of an impact.

53 Tantrums and tell-tales

Tantrums and tell-tales are generally more common among female students, but some boys do it too. I truly believe that hormones have a lot to answer for when it comes to tantrum behaviour, and girls of a certain age seem especially talented at pouting their lips and stamping their feet when they don't get their own way!

Tantrums have a terrible habit of getting out of hand very quickly, and you do not want to exacerbate the situation. Speak steadily, quietly and authoritatively, and encourage the student to take a minute to calm him or herself down and think about why they are agitated. Although your instinct may be to draw attention to their irrational behaviour, (after all, she *is* being a stroppy little madam!), it is essential you appear sympathetic and understanding without indulging the student.

Generally, if you give students enough time to cool down, and refuse to give them the negative attention they desire, they will merely nurse their pet lip for a while and then move on. Thankfully, most tantrums are very short lived and don't have to become major behaviour issues.

When a student decides to 'tell tales' on another, this can be slightly more problematic. It can sometimes be hard to establish whether or not they are telling the truth or merely trying to stir up trouble and gain a reaction from you. Don't give tell-tale behaviour any more attention than it deserves; it is a small-scale behaviour issue that generally doesn't warrant too much interest. However, if you notice it occurring frequently, it is essential that you approach the 'tell-tale' and challenge their behaviour.

 Remember: any behaviour that has a negative effect on your teaching should be dealt with accordingly. Good ground rules make for a good learning environment, but they must be adhered to.

Finally, it is not just students who have tantrums; other teachers have them too. It can be an eye-opening experience to watch a colleague have a bit of a strop, but bear in mind that it is important to support, not judge. Try to find out what the problem is, and if you can help in any way. Everyone has bad days occasionally, and it could be that this is one of theirs.

Don't forget, teachers are humans too!

54 Fighting in the corridors

Growing up can be a difficult process, and children often lack the relevant skills and abilities to deal with arguments sensibly. As a consequence, some children will express themselves physically and get into fights.

As a teacher you have a duty of care to all your students, to ensure they are kept safe and away from harm. However, this does not mean that you have to get involved with breaking up fights. Some schools even have designated patrol staff who can be summoned to deal with this kind of behaviour. Whether the violence is directed at another student or at you personally, always make sure you keep yourself safe.

Fights may take place both in and outside of lessons. The following checklist can be used to resolve any fight, regardless of the location.

Breaking up fights

- Assess the situation quickly and calmly and determine how safe it is for you to get involved. For example, how big are the students? Are there any weapons involved?
- Most fights can be stopped by a loud, firm voice. Give specific commands and call students by name.
- Ensure that any bystanders are moved well away.
- Get help – call for another member of staff or send a trustworthy student to fetch someone.
- If possible, determine who is the aggressor and who is the 'victim'. If you remove one, the other has no one to fight with.
- Avoid using physical force as much as possible, and be especially careful if you choose to restrain a student.
- Don't place yourself in between fighting students unless you are confident it is safe to do so.
- Report the incident both verbally and in writing, and notify relevant teachers, parents, carers, etc.

55 Chasing truants

An important part of teaching is making sure your students are actually in the class! Official truancy figures fluctuate widely, but it is estimated that between 50,000 and 65,000 students skip school every day. The UK government introduced truancy fines in 2004, meaning that parents can be fined up to £100 if their children are constantly absent from school.

Truancy rates increase with student age, with around 20 per cent of secondary age students playing truant at some stage in their education. However, primary school students are also noted to have a high percentage of absences, with parents actually keeping their children away from school for various reasons.

There are many reasons that a child may choose to truant from school.

- Poor relationships with teachers or a low enjoyment of school and learning
- Boredom and dissatisfaction with the curriculum
- Peer pressure or the influence of friends
- Family problems or parental attitudes
- Bullying
- Health issues or learning difficulties

Truancy should always be dealt with sensitively. Before you approach a student about their absence, ensure you have gone through the correct school procedure. Many schools have designated truancy officers working within the school who will address the problem.

If the problem is an ongoing one, it is important that parents or carers are informed and consulted, in line with anti-truancy procedures. Continued absence of young students may indicate a problem at home, as parental control is generally greater, and they may actually be supporting or causing the truancy.

When approaching older students, give them the chance to explain why they feel the need to play truant, and listen to their feelings. Some children simply cite that they are bored with school or just don't like certain lessons, and this reason should be given the same validity as a student citing bullying or peer pressure.

Be aware: any barrier that prevents a student from gaining their right to education, even if that barrier appears to be self-inflicted, should be assessed and removed.

Even More Troublesome Times

56 When they just won't get on with their work

Keeping students on task and interested can be a real challenge, especially if the subject matter isn't very stimulating or interesting to them. On average, we can concentrate solidly on a task for around 15 to 20 minutes before our attention begins to stray. Children with a learning disorder may only be able to hold their concentration for half that amount of time.

Good teaching practice suggests that around 10 to 20 minutes spent on one specific topic is just enough to hold student interest. Keeping a student motivated and on task is linked to your monitoring and assessment skills as a teacher.

Top tips for encouraging motivation and concentration

- Ensure that students feel properly involved in the lessons.
- Make the learning process fun and enjoyable.
- Be a positive and enthusiastic teacher.
- Use a variety of teaching styles and learning resources.
- Create a positive learning environment.
- Ensure that lessons are varied and stimulating.
- Give frequent, positive and accessible feedback.
- Provide opportunities for success.
- Value the students' contributions and opinions.
- Help students to find personal meaning in what they are learning, and understand the bigger picture of education.
- Provide opportunities for students to take ownership of their learning.

Even the best teacher can lose the interest of their class occasionally. You could simply demand their attention by giving a clear command, but for variation why not try one of these different ideas?

- A non-verbal signal such as raising your arm, pointing or standing on one leg will pique their interest and quieten a noisy class.
- Using visual aids such as colour-coded cards to indicate your expectations, for example red = stop what you are doing, amber = you are getting too noisy.

- Writing the names of any students who are not on task on the board – they will soon question why they have been singled out, thus redirecting their attention back to you.
- Having a 'minutes wasted' box on the board – every time you feel you are not being listened to or the class goes off task, add another minute to the box. A penalty can be enforced if you wish: for example, every minute wasted in class is a minute the class must work in complete silence.
- Pausing, looking and waiting for longer than is really necessary will make it clear that you expect everyone to be on task and listening before you continue.
- If you are using an interactive whiteboard or overhead projector, consider the use of an 'attention banner' – a bright and colourful random image or phrase (it does not have to be linked to the subject matter) that can be displayed quickly on-screen. This will prompt students to query the image, bringing their attention back to you.

Remember: once you have gained their attention you only have a short space of time in which to keep it – ensure commands and instructions are clear and concise, don't waffle!

57 The dog ate my homework

At some point in their career, every teacher will hear the age-old homework excuses. Whether it is because it has been forgotten, lost or simply not done, students can be remarkably inventive when it comes to explaining the absence of homework. Of course, you will also come across the sullen yet straightforward 'I ain't done it, Miss', often accompanied by a non-committal shrug.

How you deal with absent homework can be very indicative of what kind of teacher you are. You might be prepared to give your students chances to resubmit: or perhaps you prefer to administer immediate punishments such as detention. The severity of the penalty may also depend on the importance of the piece – for example, GCSE course-work should be chased up with more severity than a standard vocabulary exercise.

 Remember: some students are much better than others at organizing their time and motivating themselves. Occasionally their excuses really are genuine, so do try to be sympathetic. Over time you will get very accustomed to recognizing which students have genuinely forgotten, and which ones just can't be bothered!

Common excuse number 1 *'I didn't get it.'*
This can be a double-barrelled excuse. It can mean that the student did not actually receive the set homework, or they did not understand it. Always give yourself plenty of time to explain what is required and ask if everyone understands what is expected of them. Make sure you check that everyone has the required materials before they leave the class.

Common excuse number 2 *'I didn't know it had to be in today.'*
Every student should have some form of homework diary or planner in which they can mark down the task and the date it is due. Ensure every student completes this before they leave your class.

Common excuse number 3 *'I've forgotten it.'*
Sometimes this is a genuine reason, but for many it can simply be a handy get-out. Possible courses of action include telling the student that he or she has until the following day to present it to you or you will impose sanctions, or setting a detention during which the student must do the work.

Common excuse number 4   *'My printer ran out of ink/paper/blew up'* or *'My PC crashed and lost all my work.'*

In the age of the home computer, students have become very adept at using technological failures to excuse absent homework. As with Common excuse number 3, this can be a genuine excuse. Go with your instinct and either allow extra time to do it, or impose sanctions.

Common excuse number 5   *'It got wet/damaged/destroyed/thrown away by accident/my sister took it by mistake'* or *'My dog/cat/goldfish ate it.'*

If you were to believe your students, the number of terrible things that can happen to homework is remarkable – it is amazing that any homework ever gets handed in at all! You will soon become very efficient at spotting those who have real excuses and those who simply couldn't be bothered. As above, trust your instincts, and deal with the problem as you see fit.

58 The classroom is like a zoo!

Some classes simply won't sit down and get on, and insist on 'playing up'. This kind of behaviour isn't always linked to poor classroom management – it can also be due to other factors. The lesson they have prior to yours will have a direct effect on their concentration spans and hyperactivity levels. Unfortunately, once they have been dismissed from that lesson and sent to yours, it is up to *you* to calm them down.

Top tips for calming a class

- Always meet your class at the door: that way you can ensure they enter your classroom in a calm and controlled manner.
- Start by addressing the whole class in a calm, firm and authoritative manner and demand their full attention. For example, *'I want everyone to stop what they are doing and focus on me, now.'*
- Assess and monitor the class and give praise to those students who are calm and ready to work.
- Refuse to begin or continue with your lesson until everyone is calm and quiet.
- Approach disruptive students directly and call them by name.
- Think yoga: use deep breathing or muscle-stretching exercises to calm and focus a class – these work best with younger students, but can benefit older ones too.
- Consider the seating arrangements of the class – don't be afraid to move students around if you think it will improve their productivity.
- Use starters and quick quizzes to gain attention and focus, and encourage students to get on task straight away.
- If the disruption is due to violent or potentially dangerous behaviour, ensure the rest of the class is kept safe while you resolve the problem as quickly as possible.

59 Teaching outside school

Work experience, after school clubs, 'adventure' days and field trips are extra parts to teaching that are also essential parts of the curriculum. If your class is scheduled to take part in an out-of-school activity, it is highly likely that you will be expected to help supervise.

Out of school events don't have to be a worry, provided that both you and your students are well aware of what is expected. This means that behaviour policies within the classroom also apply outside it and, as their teacher, you are still in control of the class. As with any extracurricular activity, ensure you know exactly what is due to occur. Always plan for the unexpected!

Top tips

- Write a detailed checklist to go over on the day, as well as a list of all students involved.
- 'Brief' the students on details of the event, what they will be expected to do and how they should behave. Make it very clear that any unacceptable behaviour will not be tolerated and will be dealt with accordingly.
- If the activity involves a class visit, check that the coach is booked, tickets have been bought, permission slips have been signed, etc.
- For events such as work experience, make sure you know who is based where, and that any relevant contact details have been checked, etc.
- Plan ahead and consider any potential problems, such as lost wellingtons, forgotten lunches, unsuitable attire, etc.
- Take frequent registers or head-counts and make sure no one wanders off. Alert other members of staff immediately if a student goes missing.
- Ensure all students know where they should go if they get lost or split up from the group. Set definite timescales for returning to coaches, meeting for lunch, etc.
- Ensure appropriate provisions have been made for students with specific medical requirements (diabetics, asthmatics, epileptics, etc.).
- Consider health and safety and first aid requirements – remember your duty of care. Consider doing a 'risk assessment' for the activity if necessary.
- Have contact and emergency numbers to hand. Take a fully charged mobile phone with you and ensure you can contact and be contacted at all times.

60 Never work with children and animals

For most students, particularly younger ones, field trips are a real treat. Quite frequently, a field trip means paying a visit to Mother Nature and experiencing the flora and fauna of the countryside. Visits to farms, zoos, woodland and the beach are all excellent learning opportunities for your students, but can be a real headache for teachers. As the comedian W. C. Fields allegedly said, 'Never work with children or animals.' Putting the two together can be an interesting, if sometimes chaotic, experience.

Top tips

- It is essential that ground rules are in place before any trip even begins. Ensure that all your students are clear on what is acceptable behaviour and how they will be expected to act while out of school.
- Explain the potential dangers of being around animals, and how the students should act, for example keeping fingers away from bars; no feeding, teasing or otherwise upsetting the animals; ensuring their natural habitat is not disturbed, etc.
- Encourage students to explore nature responsibly, for example, highlight the importance of the Country Code; ensure all litter is picked up; encourage students to respect their surroundings.
- If the students are to collect samples of any kind, ensure these are collected carefully and with minimum disruption to the natural surroundings. Ensure insects, amphibians or any other living creatures are disrupted for the minimum amount of time and are replaced where they were found.
- Many zoos and petting farms allow children to touch the animals under the supervision of official staff. Before any student is given this opportunity, they must fully understand that this is a privilege and they must behave accordingly.
- Be fully aware of the potential hazards that may occur while outdoors, and monitor all students closely. There should be an ample number of staff present to ensure the safety of every child.

Remember: for some children a field trip may be the first experience they have had of the countryside or of seeing some animals close up. Be aware that some students may get very over-excited!

61 He said, she said: Dealing with rumours

All students love rumours, particularly 'juicy' or possibly scandalous ones. As a teacher, you can be particularly vulnerable to rumours due to your position within the school. Rumours are like bushfires; once they begin they can be very hard to stop. All you can really hope for is to try and stop them spreading.

Not all rumours are nasty though; indeed some can even work to your advantage. I found that by starting a rumour myself that I had a brown belt in karate meant that I was given a new level of respect from unruly students!

Students also love gossiping about other students. The playground grapevine is full of intriguing tales of 'what Emma Smith supposedly did with Tommy Johnson at the weekend'. Be alert for any potentially damaging or hurtful rumours, as these are a form of bullying and should be approached and dealt with promptly.

Notes, graffiti and 'Chinese whispers' regarding particular students or staff should also be removed and the perpetrator admonished. Even if it feels like a bit of harmless gossip, always consider how you would feel if it were directed at you.

If a rumour or piece of gossip does start about you, take care to keep calm and don't let it upset you. It is unlikely that the rumour is due to any personal dislike or real desire to hurt you. Sadly, some children can be very malicious and vindictive without considering the implications. If the rumours give you any real concerns – for example, the subject matter is potentially damning or could be construed as a real slur on your profession – always ensure you tell a colleague and ask for advice on how best to stamp it out.

Top tips

- Never give fuel to the fire and react to a rumour, even if it is to deny it.
- Tactically ignore direct questions or attempts to engage your attention.
- Never be tempted to comment on rumours about students or other members of staff.
- When dealing with rumours, don't make any assumptions about who said what. What was said is not as important as how it will be dealt with.

Be aware: rumours may be spread verbally or through writing. In addition to notes and graffiti, electronic formats such as email and SMS text messages may be used to spread malicious gossip. It is impossible to monitor or censor all these formats, so try to exercise damage limitation rather than resorting to Big Brother-style monitoring tactics.

62 But Mr Robinson said . . .

Occasionally you may find that you are being 'played off' against another teacher. Perhaps you are a new teacher who is being compared to an experienced one, or you could be an experienced teacher who is being compared to a new, more 'cool' member of staff.

It can be an awkward experience to find that you are being compared to your peers, especially if the comparison isn't a favourable one. You may feel hurt or upset that your students have passed judgement on you. You may not understand why you are being perceived as being a lesser teacher or person.

Other forms of 'playing off' include having your authority questioned, or compared to that of another teacher. If your colleague allows students to choose where they sit, while you impose seating plans, your decision may be questioned. This is doubly awkward if you are covering for said colleague.

Whether the problem is due to your expectations in class or of your students, always stick to your ground rules.

> In my first teaching job I was constantly plagued with one particular class of students informing me that 'Mr Jackson lets me do it' and 'Mr Jackson said we can', whenever I tried to impose my class rules. Tired of being constantly compared to Mr Jackson, I found him and discussed my concerns with him, only to find that he had done or said nothing of the sort! The next time I met the class, Mr Jackson gave them a talking-to for five minutes, leaving them with no doubt that they had been rumbled!
>
> *John, Head of Geography (47)*

Top tips if you think you are being 'played off'

- Keep confident in yourself – it is natural that students will compare you to other teachers, just as they will prefer some teachers to others.
- Stick to your own ground rules, regardless of what other teachers do.
- Refuse to be drawn in when students compare you to another teacher.
- Do not feel that you have to change in any way just because a class doesn't think you are 'as good' or 'as nice' as another teacher.

- If a student informs you that another teacher has said something, take those claims with a pinch of salt – if possible, check with that particular teacher before you react.
- Do not encourage students' doubts in other teachers – keep professional and supportive of your colleagues, whatever your personal opinions of them are!

63 Personal insults

Just as you cannot expect to get on with everyone you meet, you cannot expect to be liked by every student you teach. However, when a simple personality clash becomes more personal, and you are the victim of a verbal attack by a student, you do need to take it seriously.

Insults can range from the rude or cheeky, such as telling a teacher to 'go away', to those involving swearing, racism or derogatory comments based on the teacher's appearance, gender, etc.

 Be aware: studies by teaching unions show that many teachers suffer a daily torrent of verbal abuse, foul language and personal abuse. You do not have to put up with it!

Make it known that you operate a Zero Tolerance policy on verbal abuse or bad language, and set definite sanctions for dealing with this behaviour. Ensure that your classes are familiar with this policy and are clear what you will and will not put up with.

As when dealing with any unwanted behaviour, keep calm and don't react on a personal level, however angry or upset the student has made you feel. Verbal insults are usually a form of power-seeking or revenge-seeking behaviour. The student may be 'testing the waters' to see how far he or she can push you. Older students are more likely to use swearing to try to goad you into reacting.

Tell the student firmly that this kind of language or way of speaking is not acceptable and you will not tolerate it. You may wish to request an apology, and if (a genuine) one is forthcoming, it is good practice to accept it and move on.

If the student does not show any remorse or if the abuse is escalating, continue to be assertive, but not aggressive. Never stoop to the student's level and respond with your own insults. If necessary, give the student a time-out to allow him or her to calm down. Give the student the opportunity to take responsibility for the behaviour and amend it. Say that you need him or her to think before speaking, and that this language is getting him or her into more trouble.

It is important that verbal insults are punished, in order to enforce your Zero Tolerance policy. While you can tactically ignore many silly remarks or impulsive insults, be clear on what you expect from your students in order to encourage an environment of mutual respect and trust.

Remember: most verbal abuse and insults from students are off-the-cuff remarks and are not part of any deep-rooted resentment or hatred.

64 'I'm going to get you!' – Threats and violence

Much more serious than verbal insults are threats of physical violence against you. These are more common among older students, but even younger children may resort to threatening behaviour.

Empty threats are often said in anger, such as 'If you come near me I'll kill you!': while they can come as a surprise, these are generally not considered to be a real worry. Once the student has calmed down, the threat has invariably been forgotten.

Other threats may be far more serious and may be part of some physical intimidation. Threats that outline some specific action such as 'I'm going to petrol bomb your car' or 'I'm going to stab you after school' should be taken very seriously and referred to senior management staff.

If you feel scared or worried by a student's behaviour at any time, remove yourself from the situation and tell a colleague. Never put yourself in a situation where you may be alone with that student, and never threaten him or her back.

 Remember: although these kinds of threats are made far too often, very few of them are ever actually carried out, despite what the media would have us believe!

Top tips for dealing with violent behaviour

- If you feel unsafe, get out of the situation immediately and call another member of staff to help you.
- Stay as calm as possible. Attempt to gain control of the situation.
- Reassure the student that you understand his or her distress and wish to resolve the issue.
- Never get into a one-to-one situation in a closed room. Place yourself as close as possible to an available exit.
- Always stay in an open area, preferably with an object such as a table separating you both.
- Never grab, push or slap the student. You may defend yourself against a physical attack but you must only use acceptable force.
- If the student is shouting, ask them to lower their voice and calm down. Never shout back at the student.

- Be aware of your movements and body language. Do not make any sudden or potentially threatening motions, which may be misinterpreted.
- Write an incident report as soon as you can. Notify other teachers, parents, etc.

65 Serious accusations

It is estimated that around 400 complaints and accusations are made each year against teachers, with over three-quarters of these being found to be false. Many of these allegations are a result of teachers simply breaking up fights or giving punishments to students for unacceptable behaviour.

Teachers are particularly vulnerable to false accusations because of the varied nature of their jobs and the large numbers of young people they work with every day. Sadly, many students have no problem in making a false claim about a teacher they dislike.

Examples of serious allegations include:

- Accusing a teacher of any form of sexual abuse or improper contact with a student, or of making any sexual remarks, jokes or comments.
- Accusations of physical abuse or violence towards a student that cannot be justified as 'reasonable force'.
- Racist or religious slurs, or any other offensive language or comments directed at a student.
- Allegations relating to a teacher's skills, competency and professional behaviour, for example, being drunk or under the influence of drugs.

 Be aware: once a serious allegation has been made, it must be properly investigated. Teachers will be suspended while the investigation takes place. For many teachers, even if the allegation is proved to be completely false, the fact that it has been made will taint their reputation. It is often assumed that the fact an accusation has been made is proof enough of a teacher's guilt.

Every effort should be made to preserve the teacher's anonymity while an allegation is being investigated. The media or local press should not be given any details until the case is fully resolved.

If you are the victim of a serious allegation, you should still expect the support and understanding of your work place. If the allegation is true it is better to admit to it straight away and seek legal advice rather than lie about it. Be honest about what has happened and accept full responsibility for your actions.

What to do if you are falsely accused

- Ensure you get some legal support straight away.
- Contact your Trade Union or Citizens Advice Bureau for advice. The NASUWT and ATL teaching unions have special advisors who can help you deal with false claims.
- Search online for support groups who can help and support you, such as FACT, the association for Falsely Accused Carers and Teachers. (www.factuk.org).
- Gather as much evidence as you can to contest the allegation. Make a list of students, staff and other colleagues who may be able to act as witnesses for your defence.
- Although false allegations are very damaging to any teacher, don't lose heart. You don't have to give up on your career just because of one malicious claim.

Being Part of the Team

66 When your department hates you

You can't expect to get on with everyone you work with all the time. But what should you do if you really don't get on with your department?

Since teaching is seen to be a team-based profession, it can be a shock to realize that it is also very cliquey! This isn't a bad thing if you manage to find yourself within the clique, but is more difficult if you find yourself being pushed out. New arrivals to the school, or young teachers who haven't had the chance to build up their reputation yet, are under pressure to find their feet very quickly with both students and staff.

What many teachers find is that initial impressions from their job interview don't necessarily match the way things are done in practice. For example, you may find some department policies are outdated or just plain strange, and you may want to introduce new ways of doing things.

Sometimes, for no real reason, you just don't get on with someone in your department. However, it is essential you still maintain a professional attitude, whatever your opinions of someone!

I had been teaching at a 'challenging' school for over six years when the department head was replaced by someone younger and supposedly with a more 'dynamic' way of thinking. In reality she ended up being an idealistic, power-suited businesswoman who tried to run the department like a corporation and didn't seem to have the first clue about how to deal with the students. After a few weeks of suffering, the rest of the department had to take her to one side and explain that as interesting as her ideas were, they simply would not work in our type of school. She decided to leave her position by Christmas!

Derek, Head of Year 8 and English teacher (57)

What to do if you find tension in your department

- Accept that you can't get on with everyone. If you try too hard to please people you will only end up coming across as a sycophant.

117

- Don't be too pushy – just because people are not immediately receptive to your ideas doesn't mean they won't change their minds later. It may take time for people to adjust to your way of thinking.
- You don't have to only be friends with people in your own department – gain support and advice from other teachers across the school.
- It will take time to build up a good reputation. Be confident in your own skills and achievements and don't be disheartened just because you're not 'one of the group' straight away.
- Seek help from appropriate senior colleagues if you really feel that there are major problems with members of your department: for example, if they do not include you in major decisions, fail to support you or criticize your abilities.

67 When senior teachers fight back!

Worse than having personal problems with your department can be having issues with a senior member of staff. If you are a new or young teacher, this kind of problem can seem very overwhelming and possibly even worrying – after all, you frequently look to senior members of staff for support and advice. However, regardless of how senior they may be, or how many years of teaching experience they have, this does not give them the right to undermine or unfairly criticize you.

 Remember: members of senior staff are pretty much constantly on the go, and don't always have the time for long conversations or general chitchat. What you may perceive as rudeness or unfriendliness may simply be because they are stressed out and busy. When they have the time to sit down and discuss any problems with you, you may find that they are actually very pleasant and supportive.

If you are concerned by a senior staff member's attitude towards you, don't be afraid to approach them and try to resolve the problem. It is better to speak out honestly and openly than suffer in silence. In most cases the staff member may not even be aware they have upset or offended you.

If their behaviour continues to give you cause for concern, or you feel you are being treated unfairly or inadequately, you may wish to consider making an official complaint to a member of staff higher up, or to your Local Education Authority.

 Be aware: never be afraid to stand up for your rights if you feel your career is being affected detrimentally. (See Calamity 76, 'Beating the Bullies', for how to deal with senior tyrants.)

68 Keeping your Head of Department sweet

Your Head of Department is an important part of your working life – they oversee many important decisions within the department and act as part of the middle management in the school management structure.

In addition to managing departmental educational, they are also expected to manage people – the subject teachers within their department. Teachers who apply for general classroom practitioner jobs generally meet their prospective Heads of Department during the interview process.

Middle managers have a wide variety of job responsibilities, including teaching, monitoring, departmental assessment and leading the department as a professional. Middle-management decisions can alter how a department is run and can also affect the whole school.

It is always advantageous to ensure your Head of Department likes you, not just as a teacher, but also as a person. Department decisions will affect your working role, so it is good practice to take an active interest in how the department operates, and contribute to the decision-making process. By doing so, not only can you validate yourself as a good team player, you can also improve your understanding of management policies, and expand your career direction.

Top ten ways to impress your Head of Department

1 Take the time to chat to your Head of Department and get interested in them as a person.
2 Show that you are keen and enthusiastic by accepting more responsibilities.
3 Become an excellent team player – pitch in and be a part of a solution.
4 Meet your deadlines – ensure paperwork, marking and reports are up to date.
5 Start or take over an extracurricular activity such as a club or after-school sport.

6 Take the initiative – be seen to solve problems on your own as much as you can.

7 A little politeness can go a long way – always greet people with a smile and a friendly word.

8 Dress, act and speak professionally – make an effort to be a 'model' teacher.

9 Learn a new skill and share it with your colleagues.

10 Have excellent time-keeping skills and a flexible approach to your work.

69 Avoiding cliques

If you thought that cliques were just part of the school playground, think again. Perhaps it is due to the type of working environment in school, or maybe the behaviour of the students affects staff more than they realize – whatever the reason, cliques are a common staffroom occurrence.

It is not just newcomers who have to battle cliques: even teachers who have been at the same school for years can feel isolated and pushed out of these select groups. It seems that whatever we teach our students about acceptance and friendship, we often fail to put into practice in the staffroom.

Cliques can be based on any factor that differentiates people from one another. This may be as simple as age and gender, or social habits. There are no real rules for gaining a place in a clique – the kinds of alienation we may have experienced as children can also follow us into adulthood. Even as grown-ups we may begin to ask, 'But *why* don't they like me?'

Cliques can be positive things; a group of people with similar interests who band together will also share ideas and strategies. However, cliques can also be destructive or exclusive, and those outside the group may be denied important information or professional support.

It is difficult, if not impossible, to eliminate cliques completely. Senior staff may wish to discourage cliques if they feel they are affecting the unity of the teaching team. Members of cliques may however resist change and merely band together more tightly.

 Remember: teachers who are incredibly popular with their students will not necessarily be equally popular with staff. Although it may seem hurtful, or bewildering, try not to take it personally. Concentrate on making a few close friends rather than trying to be accepted into a clique.

Being an NQT can be very stressful – you have lots of demands put on you and you have a lot of pressure to prove yourself. Staffroom cliques are particularly difficult, you have no idea of the dynamics or politics of each department or who you can go to talk to if you have a problem. It can be quite alienating and depressing at first, and for the first few weeks I sat on my own in the staffroom. Eventually one of the Maths teachers took pity on me and started chatting to me one day. By the end of the week, more people had come to sit with us and we had accidentally formed our own little clique!

I make loads of effort to welcome new teaching students and NQT's now; I know how awful it feels when no one talks to you.

Vicky, Science teacher (25)

70 There is no 'I' in 'team'

Being a team player is important when you are a teacher. Even when you have been at a school for a while, it is essential you keep up with what's going on. Although some teachers are often tempted to do their own thing, and can get quite protective of their teaching methods and resources, the more you share, the less you have to do!

 Remember: team teaching, group planning and departmental assessment strategies are all excellent ways of cutting down your workload. Teachers who are willing to work together and share their schemes of work or lessons ideas are also teachers who are less stressed and have more free time.

Many departments pool their teaching resources and work out long-term schemes of work before each new school year. This has the benefit of ensuring teachers can support each other throughout the scheme. They can share resources and teaching tips and, in the event of absences, cover is much easier to arrange. Sharing resources also cuts down on the amount of paper and photocopying needed, reducing departmental costs. The added advantage for new teachers is that they do not need to spend lots of time developing and planning lesson resources.

Even if your school doesn't follow this kind of policy, you can still share your teaching resources and helpful tips with your department, and encourage others to do the same. As the saying goes, 'two heads are better than one', and it can make planning and preparation a whole lot more fun if you bounce ideas off your colleagues.

Being a valued member of the team also means you don't alienate yourself from your peers. If you have a sociable working environment where you feel friends, not just co-workers, surround you, you will also feel happier, be more productive and truly enjoy your job.

71 Your reputation with staff

Just as important as your reputation with students is your reputation with staff. Both as a new or experienced teacher, your colleagues will frequently make on-the-spot decisions about you based on how you behave and respond. They may have also heard gossip about you from your previous workplace or former colleagues.

Gaining a good reputation among your peers is not always straight-forward. While a long list of impressive qualifications may gain you the respect of your fellow professionals, it won't necessarily mean you are liked as a person. Your professional reputation may also differ from your personal one: for example, you may have an amazing teaching ability, but a very poor sense of humour.

 Remember: a truly great teacher doesn't need to court popularity – it will come to him or her. In comparison, the best way to build a good reputation is to be honest, open and friendly, and show willing to become an integral part of the school.

Things that will gain you a bad reputation

- Gossiping or making judgemental comments about other teachers.
- Being two-faced or hypocritical in your relationships with other teachers.
- 'Bitching' or bad-mouthing staff, especially to students.
- Shirking responsibilities or being lazy.
- Constant absences or 'pulling a sickie'.
- Being frequently late and leaving early.
- Undermining other members of staff.

72 Avoiding the 'doormat' problem

Starting a job at a new school, either as a new or experienced teacher, can be quite challenging. Not only will you feel the pressures of having to prove yourself in a new environment, you will also most likely want to be accepted as soon as possible as a team member.

Many new or young teachers end up doing too much to try to be liked. They are often unsure how to assert themselves, especially when dealing with more experienced staff members, and as a result are over keen. While sticking your neck out and being willing to do more than your share shows dedication, it can also mean that you stretch yourself too thin. Every teacher's workload is large, but for an NQT or young teacher in the early stages of their career, there may be added pressures to perform to high standards.

What is essential is that you are doing your job to the best of your ability – regardless of how popular you may be among students and staff. If you begin to adopt the 'can-do' attitude too much, you may find that people merely take you for granted. For example, volunteering to help out with after school clubs is both beneficial to your career and to your reputation. Offering to help out with too many after school clubs will just mean that you leave yourself with far less free time and risk pushing yourself to exhaustion.

Similarly, do not feel like you *have* to accept further responsibilities just to become part of the team. If your colleagues think less of you because you decline to help out with Year 9's ballet production, remember this is their problem not yours. Providing you are fulfilling your role as a teacher and giving your best, you should never feel like you have to impress people just to be accepted into the crowd.

Top tips to avoid becoming a 'doormat'

- Learn to say 'no'. If you are being asked to do far more jobs than your peers, it is reasonable to suspect you are being taken advantage of.
- Don't feel pressured to act in certain ways just to gain popularity – your personality is separate to your teaching ability.
- Avoid becoming a 'Yes Man'. Stand up for your rights and beliefs – don't be afraid to disagree or offer a different opinion.

- While older members of staff may have more years of teaching experience, this does not mean they are better *people* than you. Give your peers the respect they deserve for their achievements, but remember you have your own to be proud of too.

73 Socializing with staff

A lot of teachers socialize together and become good friends. Some even find romance and end up married! The team-based nature of the job means that people often band together to help each other. There can be an overwhelming sense of camaraderie between departments and, in some cases, a strong notion of 'it's us against them'. Due to the many potential difficulties and pitfalls of the job, knowing you have a good support network around you can be a real blessing.

Thanks to this team spirit, genuine, solid friendships can thrive. There are a lot of opportunities to discuss ideas and strategies with your colleagues, and as a by-product of this, more chances to be sociable. It is unsurprising that many departmental meetings conclude with tea and biscuits and a chat, while teachers wind down and relax with each other.

However, there are times when being friends with your co-workers can land you in muddy waters. While the profession may perhaps feel more friendly and open than some other types of employment, never make the mistake of saying too much. Just as you wouldn't let the students know details of your private life, don't feel you should tell the staff either!

Many new teachers make the mistake of being too open in the staffroom – a mistake which often comes back to bite them when they realize that they have said too much. People will always judge you, there is no real way of avoiding that fact: but it is sensible not to give them too much information to judge you with.

For example, if you spend your weekends partying at a local nightclub, and drinking until dawn, that is your business and there is nothing wrong with that. Be aware, however, some other members of staff may consider your behaviour to be less than professional and their opinion of you may change.

 Remember: be honest and open, but don't tell people what they do not need to know. To be blunt, you are employed to be an education professional five days in every week. As long as you uphold standards of a positive role model for your students, your private life is your own.

Even trickier can be staff social events such as Christmas, New Year or an end-of-term 'do'. When the alcohol is flowing, you may find your mouth is a little loose. Be especially careful of what you say when under the influence of alcohol, especially if it is overly honest, flirtatious or potentially damaging to your career! Many teachers have had their staffroom reputation ruined by a little too much vodka and not enough tact.

I had always got on really well with my Head of Department and enjoyed chatting to her in the staffroom. One weekend, I went to my university reunion party and got rather drunk. I ended up getting rather 'friendly' with an old friend, which ended up being a complete disaster. I made the mistake of telling people on the Monday, thinking it was just a bit of funny story. Unfortunately my devoutly Catholic Head of Department didn't find it so funny, and spent the rest of the term pretty much avoiding me as much as she could!

Jennifer, Primary teacher (27)

74 The (dreaded) Christmas party

Everyone knows someone who once got incredibly drunk at the staff Christmas party, blasted out a tuneless rendition of 'I Will Survive' on the karaoke machine, and then passionately kissed the Head of Geography underneath the mistletoe. It is all terribly amusing – unless that person happens to be you!

The etiquette of how to behave at a staff social is always under some scrutiny in any working environment, but for teachers it can seem a lot worse. You have to face your colleagues the next Monday, and they may well have formed new opinions of you based on your behaviour. Somehow the students always seem to find out about your indiscretions (although how this is so is a mystery, as no teacher would ever admit to be so indiscreet as to tell the students the juicy details!). You have to face the Head of Geography while sober. You will most likely be the subject of staffroom gossip and jokes for a while. None of this is very pleasant, especially if you are still in your first term as an NQT!

However, as I have said many times before, teachers are humans too, and as such behave in unpredictable and silly ways occasionally. Providing you do not do anything to truly jeopardize your career, embarrass the school or behave unprofessionally in front of your students, a little bit of drunken frivolity is acceptable. To repeat myself yet again: even teachers are entitled to have a life!

Top ten things to avoid doing at the staff Christmas party

1 Consuming too much alcohol – drink sensibly and avoid getting drunk.
2 Accepting, offering or otherwise participating in the taking of any illegal substance. Not only is this an issue of the law, it is a potential cause for a disciplinary.
3 Having a go on the karaoke machine (unless you really can sing!).
4 Getting a bit too 'friendly' with any of your colleagues, or behaving too provocatively.
5 Utilizing the reprographics equipment for any 'humorous' purposes!

6 Dancing on the tables.
7 Air guitar.
8 Trying to matchmake your colleagues – it is best to leave well alone!
9 Gossiping, bad-mouthing or passing judgement on any member of staff or student.
10 Inappropriate dress.

Finding Support

75 Help! I need somebody!

There may come a time in your professional life when things do get on top of you and everything seems a bit too much. It is only to be expected in some cases, especially if you have a heavy workload to deal with. Not everyone gets huge amounts of support in their school, regardless of whether they need it or not.

 Remember: accepting that you need help is not a sign of weakness or failure. It takes a stronger person to accept they need support than to struggle on in misery.

While ideally you should talk to your colleagues, Head of Department or whoever you feel you can trust, the reality is that many teachers don't feel comfortable telling their peers that they are struggling. Even if they do decide to tell someone within the school, the level of support they receive as a consequence is not always of a great standard.

The Teacher Support Network (www.teachersupport.info) is a national charity. It is an excellent place to get free and confidential support and advice, and has been endorsed by the NASUWT. Their helpline (08000 562 561) is open 24 hours a day, 365 days a year. You do not need to be a member of a teaching union to be eligible for their services. The Association of Teachers and Lecturers (www.atl.org.uk) has a number of crisis and support helplines which are also open 24/7, and manned by professionals.

If you are having problems finding inspiration for planning lessons, there is a whole wealth of brilliant websites designed for teachers, with many tried-and-tested ideas for you to access and use.

Top teaching resource websites

- BBC Schools – www.bbc.co.uk/schools/teachers
- Chalkface – www.chalkface.com
- Curriculum Online – www.curriculumonline.gov.uk
- Learnthings – www.learnthings.co.uk
- Primary Resources – www.primaryresources.co.uk
- Schoolzone – www.schoolzone.co.uk
- Teachernet – www.teachernet.gov.uk
- Teacher Resource Exchange – http://tre.ngfl.gov.uk
- Teachit – www.teachit.co.uk
- TES Resource Bank – www.tes.co.uk/resources
- Top Marks – www.topmarks.co.uk

76 Beating the bullies

Sadly, bullying does go on even in the best of schools, and it's not just the students who get bullied. Many teachers complain of bullying and harassment at work from other members of staff. Although teaching is supposed to be a team profession, many teachers (especially new or younger ones) are often bullied or made to feel inadequate by their colleagues. One in three teachers claims to have been subject to some form of bullying at work.

Bullying is all about control, and many bullies are already in a position of power, which they abuse to their advantage. In adults, most bullying takes the form of long-term psychological attrition. Constant, trivial criticisms or refusals to value others' achievements are all forms of bullying. The better the victim performs, the more the bully will judge them. Bullies may also play on insecurities or self-doubts and convince their victims that their successes are insignificant.

Most victims do nothing to attract the bullying: they can simply be in the wrong place at the wrong time, but the bully often sees them as some sort of threat. The victims are usually popular and well liked, and very good at their job. Most workplace bullies are disliked by everyone and often have poor people skills, although they can also be very charming and articulate. Many bullies are emotionally or professionally insecure, but may exhibit arrogance and refuse to admit they are in the wrong.

Bullies are often in a high position of authority over their victims. This means that most grievance procedures are meant to be conducted directly through them, which frequently suppresses most potential complaints or discourages victims from making a complaint at all.

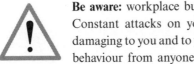 **Be aware:** workplace bullying should never be ignored. Constant attacks on your self-esteem or self-worth is damaging to you and to your career, and is not acceptable behaviour from anyone. Many victims worry that they will not be taken seriously or will exacerbate the situation if they complain, and it is this fear that many bullies play on.

What to do if you believe you are being bullied at work

- Get support from your family, friends and colleagues. Talk about your concerns and how it is making you feel. Keep a written record of any incidents that you believe are forms of bullying.
- Read up on your school's grievance procedures and follow the policy exactly. Every attempt should be made to resolve problems verbally in the first instance, but when this is not possible, make all complaints in writing and keep copies.
- Before you make an official complaint, put everything you want to say in order and concentrate on facts and events. Don't omit anything you may later want to bring up before a complaints board, even if it seems trivial at the time.
- Gain the support of your union and ask for advice. They will support you if you decide to make a complaint. Sometimes it is even possible to make a shared complaint with a group of teachers – this will help to validate your claims.
- Remind yourself that you are a good teacher and you have done nothing wrong. You do not deserve to be bullied. Don't let fear of repercussions prevent you from standing up for your rights.
- Be strong and don't back down just because things may get difficult or awkward. Bullies survive due to intimidation and fear, and frequently use their position of power to invalidate any claims. In reality, bullies are insecure, petty-minded and jealous people, and are certainly not worth your respect.

 Remember: those who can, do. Those who can't, bully!

77 Unions and their uses

During your initial teacher training and your induction year, you may be swamped with information and fliers inviting you to join a teaching union. There are a number of unions to choose from; who you choose is ultimately up to you. Unlike registering with the General Teaching Council (GTC), whether you are a union member or not will have no impact on your employability. You do not have any obligation to join a union, although it is generally a very good idea. A union is your professional 'insurance policy' inside the classroom.

Joining a union will give you a number of benefits:

1 Legal advice and representation should you ever need it.
2 A valuable and practical support service you can turn to if you have any queries or concerns.
3 Discounts on commercial services, such as cheaper car, home and travel insurance or credit card offers.
4 The chance to make your opinions count and be involved with national teaching issues and campaigns.
5 Trade union and professional training and information opportunities, often at a reduced cost.

Most unions will offer you free membership when you are a student, and a discounted rate during your induction year. Membership rates vary depending on how you choose to pay and at what stage you are at in your career, but you should expect to pay around £5 to £8 per month.

 Be aware: a union can only help you with problems or concerns that occurred after you joined them.

After joining a union you can expect to receive a monthly newspaper or magazine, as well as full access to members-only restricted areas on their websites. You should be advised as to who is your local union representative, and provided with contact details in case you need to request their services. You should also be kept fully up to date with changes or improvements to the union, and any campaigns or action they are undertaking on behalf of teachers.

Your union representative will be able to advise you on a number of concerns, such as pay and conditions; health and safety at work; behaviour management tips; and medical and disability issues, including stress or anxiety at work. He or she will also be able to give you legal advice and representation should you need it.

Remember: some of the larger unions have in excess of 200,000 members, and are often very busy. If you need immediate help or advice, there are a number of helpline numbers you can contact to discuss your worries.

If you are dissatisfied with your union or do not feel that they are helping or supporting you as much as you believe they should, you are entitled to make a complaint or cancel your membership.

The strength of any union lies in its members and their commitment to each other. You may find it beneficial to become more involved with your union, or even volunteer to become a union representative.

Teaching unions

United Kingdom:

- Association of School and College Leaders (ASCL) – www. ascl.org.uk
- Association of Teachers and Lecturers (ATL) – www.atl.org. uk
- National Association of Head Teachers (NAHT) – www. naht.org.uk
- National Association of Schoolmasters, Union of Women Teachers (NASUWT) – www.nasuwt.org.uk
- National Union of Teachers (NUT) – www.nut.org.uk
- Professional Association of Teachers (PAT) – www.pat.org.uk
- Society of Headmasters and Headmistresses of Independent Schools (SHMIS) – (formerly the SHA) – www.shmis.org.uk
- University and College Lecturer's Union (formerly the AUT – www.aut.org.uk – and NATFHE – www.natfhe.org.uk) – www.ucu.org.uk

Scotland:

- Educational Institute of Scotland (EIS) – www.eis.org.uk
- Headteachers' Association of Scotland (HAS) – www.has-scot-land.co.uk
- Scottish Secondary Teachers' Association (SSTA) – www.ssta. org.uk

78 Working with other schools

As we are constantly told, teaching is a team-orientated occupation. In order for strategies and policies to be the most effective possible, they need to work collaboratively across the whole school.

The Office for Standards in Education (OfSTED) frequently praise schools that are looking towards the community to help support their education system. This means that the school is not simply a closed unit where education professionals teach children the National Curriculum, but has a real impact on the social community it is based in.

One of the real tests is working with other schools within the area. Until 2005, this idea was supported by the Beacon Schools project, which has sadly now been phased out. The idea was to build partnerships between schools so that they could share their knowledge and effective strategies with others, in order to actively encourage more positive learning. The aims and initiatives behind this project are still maintained.

For secondary schools, the Leading Edge Partnership Programme offers the chance for education professionals to work together to confront the challenges many schools face. For primary schools, Primary Strategy Learning Networks (PSLNs) are being set up to help schools work together and encourage higher standards in literacy and numeracy, and to establish a wide and varied curriculum.

The benefits of working with other schools can be very great, providing everyone involved knows what they intend to get out of the partnership. It can be very easy to begin a union whereby it appears that both schools will benefit, but in reality the amount of collaboration grows thin, and the alliance occurs only in name. For a partnership to work, it is necessary to initiate and maintain positive plans, such as:

- Community-wide school meetings
- Sharing resources and strategies
- Inviting additional students to use your campus facilities
- Approaching other education professionals to share their ideas and achievements.

Linking with other schools does not have to be the responsibility of senior management or Head of Department: all teachers can get involved in promoting optimistic thinking between schools.

Rules to remember when you are working with other schools

- Always avoid the 'my school is better than your school' attitude. Treat all schools within the partnership as equals; your mission is to improve education opportunities community-wide, not to merely showcase your own school's achievements.
- Be especially clear about what you hope to get out of the partnership – it must be seen to be making a difference, not simply looking impressive on the Local Education Authority reports.
- Bring lots of ideas to the table, and be prepared to share them. Don't try to 'piggy-back' on another school's achievements; find ways of attaining them yourself.
- Be prepared to accept criticism – some schools may not find your methods or ideas to be practical and will have other ways of working. Be ready to try new ideas, regardless of your personal scepticism.

79 Personal development days and training

INSET or In-Service Training Days were introduced in the 1980s by the Conservative government's then Secretary of State, Kenneth Baker. This is why they were often referred to as 'Baker Days'. INSET days give school staff an opportunity to be together at one time, and for much of this time provide the chance to train and update skills and knowledge together.

On average, all schools hold at least five INSET day a year. Teachers are obliged to be in service for 195 days per year, out of which 190 are teaching days. INSET days are usually added to the beginning or end of teachers' school holidays, in order to minimize any disruption to termtime obligations. Legally, your attendance at INSET days is voluntary, but your presence is strongly encouraged (and frequently expected) by the school.

INSET days are arranged to help staff maintain and develop their professional skills and knowledge for whole school development planning. While many members of staff find them tedious and often boring, they are an excellent professional development aid. They may be based at the school, or you may be given the opportunity to attend a course or meeting elsewhere.

As with all training, the more you put into it, the more you will get out of it. Although you may find the prospect of INSET days somewhat off-putting or unnecessary, they can provide some excellent ideas and strategies to improve your teaching ability. Most INSET days are very informal, and can even be fun if you are prepared to explore what is offered to you.

INSET days can cover a wide variety of topics. Examples are:

- National initiatives and strategies (such as numeracy and literacy)
- Assessment and grading issues
- Curriculum planning, design and implementation
- Behaviour management strategies
- Self-assessment for teaching and learning

For NQTs, there is an additional amount of training expected of you in the form of your Career Entry and Development Profile (CEDP), which you will have first seen at the end of your ITT. The CEDP acts as an important link between your ITT, your first teaching post and your continuing professional development. It allows you to focus and reflect on your goals and your achievements at an early stage, and to discuss extra requirements to further your career. Be advised that some schools do not fully understand what benefits the CEDP can bring NQTs, and as a result you may find you need to push a little harder to get the results you want.

 Be aware: don't be afraid to ask for further training and development, at whatever stage you have reached in your career. It is your right to have a level of professional development open to you, and to be given the opportunities to progress upwards on the educational career ladder.

80 Dealing with disputes

Not everyone sees eye-to-eye on everything, and sometimes you might think your department or colleagues are wrong. Perhaps you disagree with a behaviour management policy, or believe you are being expected to do too much work. Whatever your concern, *don't let it fester!*

At some point in their career everyone goes home feeling angry and irritable, either at the way their workplace is managed or at a specific colleague. We are all guilty of 'bitching' about other people every once in a while. However, if your concern is ongoing or you feel that there has been a detrimental effect on your working ability or career path, you must address it immediately.

Approach the person involved and raise the issue with them diplomatically and calmly. Express your concerns and explain clearly why you disagree or are angry, without being unnecessarily confrontational. Listen to their response and make an effort to find a compromise. Don't be afraid to express your opinions and offer new ideas, but do accept that, due to the hierarchy within all schools, your suggestions will not always be entertained straight away.

If your attempts to alleviate your concerns are unsatisfactory and you are still dissatisfied with the actions of your Head of Department or senior management, you may find it useful to approach your union representative for advice.

 Remember: your peers in higher employment positions than your own have invariably got there through hard work and real dedication to their jobs. It is important that you respect that and value their skills. However, this does not mean they can undermine you, criticize you unnecessarily or erect barriers between you and your career progression. Always put your gripes into perspective before you jump off the deep end, but never be afraid to speak out if you think you need to.

81 Disciplinary procedures

Your school's governing body is responsible for all disciplinary and grievance procedures. Policies and guidelines should be made available to all teachers, and clearly show what is acceptable and unacceptable teacher behaviour. A disciplinary may come from within the school or from the Local Education Authority, depending on the type of concern and the member of staff involved.

Depending on the misdemeanour, teachers may be charged with:

- Misconduct – for example, not meeting acceptable teaching standards; constant lateness or unauthorized absence; verbal abuse towards students; lack in their duty of care towards students.
- Gross misconduct – for example: teaching under the influence of drink or drugs; violent behaviour to staff or students; unlawful behaviour within the school; any suggestion of sexual abuse towards their students.

A charge of misconduct will generally result in a verbal warning, rising to a written warning and possible dismissal if there is no improvement seen after a specific time period. A charge of gross misconduct will warrant an immediate written warning, rising in stages of seriousness if no improvement is seen, which may cumulate in dismissal.

In England and Wales, all qualified teachers who teach in maintained ('state') schools, pupil referral units and non-maintained special schools must be registered with the General Teaching Council (GTC). The GTC can act as a regulatory body for teachers to uphold the high standards of performance expected from all teachers. Since June 2001, the GTC has been responsible for investigating and hearing cases against registered teachers who are allegedly guilty of unacceptable professional conduct or serious professional incompetence. In serious cases, a teacher can be removed from the GTC register for a minimum of two years, during which time the teacher may not return to teaching as a profession.

Cases that involve child welfare and safety are the responsibility of the Department for Education and Skills (DfES).

 Be aware: if you are the focus of any disciplinary action, it is essential that you contact your union official for advice as soon as possible.

Assessment and Feedback

82 Dealing with 'problem' parents

Not all parents are easy to approach: in fact sometimes they can be worse to deal with than their children! Some parents simply do not seem interested in their children's education, while others are over-interested and question your every move as their teacher.

In addition to termly parents' evenings, you may find it necessary to meet with parents more frequently to discuss a student's progress. As well as you calling upon the parents, be aware they may also call on you. Whatever the issue to be discussed, always remain focused on the positives, and communicate in an open and friendly manner. Your role is to provide their child with a high standard of education, in addition to providing them with essential 'life-skills'.

Not everyone will have the same views as you on what and how to teach, and it is important you respect parental wishes and take them into consideration, as well as upholding the ethos of the school. Ultimately, it is the parent's right to determine what kind of education their child should receive, and if they are unhappy with your standard of teaching they also have every right to complain. Try not to take criticisms personally, and focus on how a compromise can best be reached. Always ensure any decisions are in the child's best interests.

In the unfortunate situation of a parent not seeming to care about their child's education, keep in mind you cannot *make* them care. Be encouraging and enthusiastic while focusing on the child's achievements. When poor behaviour is an issue, concentrate on how the behaviour contravenes school policies, rather than how the behaviour affects you personally. Clearly explain school policies and offer positive ways that the behaviour could be approached and modified at home. Never, ever criticize their parenting skills, regardless of how tempting it may be!

In some cases, the child's parents may not be allowed on site due to previous unacceptable or violent behaviour. Any dealings with these parents are best done either over the telephone or through an approved letter. In extreme cases, it may be preferable to liaise with some form of external mediator, such as a social services representative, to communicate important information. Always ask for advice before approaching a known 'problem' parent.

It is expected that all schools take a Zero Tolerance approach to any form of violence or verbal assault from parents, and in more challenging areas a good link with the local police and antisocial behaviour team is essential. If parents persist in behaving in an unacceptable way, they may even find themselves issued with an Antisocial Behaviour Order (ASBO) or restraining order, which prevents them from entering school grounds.

 Remember: verbal and physical assaults from parents are rare occurrences, and support networks are in place to deal with any problems.

The best way to gain a parent's confidence in you is to open yourself up to them. Keep regular contact with them either through letters or telephone calls, and show you are willing to consider their ideas. Regular feedback through homework diaries or report cards is a good way of keeping parents informed about what is going on.

 Be aware: don't forget, you are the qualified teacher, and as such, you are likely to know how best to deliver lesson content. Don't be bullied into changing your teaching style for just one child, but do be aware of differentiation needs.

83 'Nice to meet you, Mr Jones'

Regular parents' evenings are one of the best opportunities for teachers and parents to communicate and discuss any worries or concerns, as well as to hear about their child's achievements. However, although they are a proactive experience for all concerned, they can also be tiring and draining for everyone. Teachers frequently complain that they don't have the time to devote to in-depth interviews, and parents often feel like they have been 'fobbed off' without being able to discuss their queries in detail.

When you consider that an average core subject teacher may teach 150-plus students, it can be very difficult arranging the time to meet with every parent.

 Remember: all teachers, including NQTs, will be expected to contribute in some way to parents' evenings. Bear in mind that, as well as the child's teacher, you are also an ambassador for the school. Make sure you look the part as well as act professionally.

Some schools organize set interview times for parents, and parents' evenings may be spread out over two or more days to cover all taught years. Appointments with teachers must be made in advance, which gives the teacher a chance to prepare any relevant material to aid the discussion.

Other schools may prefer a 'drop-in' policy, where teachers are available for consultation without a prior appointment. This means the parent can see as many or as few teachers as they wish, but on a first-come-first-served basis. The danger here is that meetings can go on for a long time if time limits are not imposed on each consultation.

Parents' evenings give teachers and parents the chance to discuss a whole range of issues. Examples include talking about:

- Any strengths or weakness within a particular subject.
- Any recent school report or other teacher-to-parent feedback.
- Targets and achievements in relation to curriculum requirements, such as literacy or numeracy.
- Any noted problems or concerns within the school environment.

- Issues relating to behaviour and conduct while at school and at home.
- A child's attitude to homework or coursework, and how this could be monitored, encouraged or improved.
- How frequently and in what way teachers may contact parents to discuss any issues.
- Opportunities to share information regarding the curriculum, exam expectations, key dates, etc.
- Any other issues which parents or teachers may wish to raise.

84 Telephoning parents

Telephone calls to parents can be necessary for many reasons, and are acceptable forms of communication for both good and not-so-good news. However, sometimes they can be harder than arranged meetings. On the one hand you don't have to approach the parent face-to-face: but on the other, the call will only be as pleasant as the subject matter you are calling to discuss.

To make a telephone call to a parent as stress-free as possible, always do some preparation before you call. Even if you are merely telephoning to commend a student, be aware that the parent may use the opportunity to raise other issues with you, and it is helpful if you have the information ready to divulge.

If your call relates to some concern or problem, make sure you have all the facts and relevant verification to hand, such as detention slips, notes from the parent, coursework or homework to be discussed, etc.

Telephone calls often worry and intimidate teachers; they often feel that it is some form of confrontation and are nervous about how to approach it.

Helpful hints for telephoning parents

1   Telephone parents with good news as much as possible. This gives you a chance to introduce yourself and get to know the parent, which will make any later calls easier to do.
2   Prepare yourself before you make the call: organize a checklist that highlights what you hope to achieve. Ensure you know who you need to speak to and how to address them.
3   Be polite and professional. Identify yourself as a member of the school and state why you are calling.
4   Refer to school policies and behaviours rather than personal opinions, and offer possible solutions.
5   Give the parent the opportunity to engage – listen to their opinions and solutions. Always keep the tone calm and professional. Be diplomatic when discussing problems.
6   End the call on a positive note, and encourage parents to contact you if they need to.
7   Keep some sort of record detailing the time and date of the call, what was discussed and how issues were resolved (if appropriate).

85 Letters to parents

Most letters to parents will follow a standard format, and will be arranged and approved by a senior member of staff before they are sent out. Letters to parents usually act as a form of general communication, such as informing them of upcoming events or changes to the school calendar. They may have a tear-off slip that should be signed and returned, or simply be a bulletin to pass on essential information.

There may also be a time when you need to write to a specific parent directly. You may be concerned about a student's progress or wish to communicate sensitive information: or perhaps your attempts to contact a parent by other means have failed.

Always check school policy before sending out letters to parents. Depending on the subject matter, you may find that it is deemed inappropriate or unnecessary, especially if you are a new teacher. A senior member of staff may prefer to take responsibility for all written communication.

 Be aware: if you are sending letters home regarding detentions, behavioural issues or any other areas of concern, it is recommended that you send these letters via the postal service. Entrusting important or confidential letters to the care of the student involved will invariably mean the letter is never delivered!

Top tips for writing letters to parents

- All letters to parents from the school should be word-processed and printed on paper bearing the school's letterhead. Don't forget, by doing this, you are linking your opinions and concerns with those of the school.
- Never express a written opinion to a parent that may defame the school or otherwise damage your or the school's reputation.
- Never express a written opinion to a parent that is derogatory or insulting to them, their child, or any other topic pertaining to personal issues.
- Ensure all letters are well written, with the appropriate spelling and grammar, and are of a formal and professional tone.
- Avoid humour, sarcasm and colloquialisms, as these are too easily misinterpreted.

- Be clear and concise: don't ramble. If your letter requires a response from the parent, ensure this is made clear. Offer ways in which you can be contacted.
- Ask a colleague to check it over before you send it.

86 Detentions and punishments

One of the most popular forms of sanction used in school is the detention. In order for this to work effectively, it must be followed up, which can be very time-consuming for a teacher.

Any sanction is only as effective as the result it achieves. If you find yourself handing out detentions like sweets, but no one ever turns up, it is time to review what is going wrong! Ideally, any form of punishment should be relative to the 'crime' and follow some standard form of consequences:

Consequence 1 – First verbal warning issued, requesting a change in behaviour.
Consequence 2 – Second verbal warning, detailing what sanction can be expected if the behaviour is not modified (for example, kept back, 10-minute detention, etc.)
Consequence 3 – Sanction imposed with a further verbal warning.

I advise all teachers to create and display a behaviour checklist in their classrooms that clearly shows what is acceptable and what sanctions will be imposed if expectations are not met.

 Remember: always give the student(s) the chance to address and reform their behaviour before imposing any punishment.

Top tips on detention

- As a teacher you are legally allowed to impose a same-day detention for up to 15 minutes.
- Short, same-day detentions are generally held at break time, lunchtime or after school.
- Teachers are responsible for monitoring their own detentions – if you impose them, you must follow them up. Do not expect a colleague to hold your detentions for you!
- You must give 24 hours' notice if you intend to impose longer detentions, and the student's parents or guardians must be

151

informed. This can be arranged via a telephone call or letter/slip home.

- Department, faculty or year detentions may also be appropriate. These generally last around 30 minutes and will be monitored by an appropriate member of staff.
- For serious cases or repeat offenders, the option of senior management detentions may be considered.

Different schools will have different policies on following up non-attendance to detentions. Where possible, approach the student direct and ask them why they did not turn up before contacting parents or other members of staff. Students do forget things!

87 Giving rewards

Whenever the words 'behaviour management' are uttered, our thoughts invariably turn to how to approach poor behaviour, and how to punish those who don't behave as we would wish. We frequently forget that good behaviour management is as much dependent on rewarding good behaviour as it is about tackling bad.

To encourage good behaviour we should lead by example. The best way to approach this is to commend those who are meeting our behaviour expectations. Discipline doesn't have to be stressful or negative. Giving rewards for good behaviour is a form of discipline. Never underestimate the value of a simple 'well done' or other verbal commendation. This is a very quick form of assessment and monitoring: it boosts self-esteem and shows you are engaged with the class. Focusing more on good behaviour also means you can dilute the effect of the bad.

Recognizing and praising hard work and good behaviour, while dealing with poor behaviour in an effective and consistent way, will create a positive ethos and, in turn, a calmer learning environment.

 Remember: treat all your pupils fairly and without prejudice. Be wary of having 'favourites' or being more lenient on 'good' pupils. Treat all poor behaviour in the manner it deserves.

Top 'rewards' for students

(Not all of these rewards will be suitable for all ages. You will know which rewards are the most appropriate for your classes.)

- Verbal praise, either on a one-to-one or whole-class level.
- Coloured stars or smiley faces stuck to work or on a class chart.
- 'Smarties' – coloured paper vouchers that can be distributed as necessary to praise good behaviour.
- Commendations in the form of merits, class points or house points. (Many schools give students the opportunity to gain merit certificates after a certain number have been collected.)
- 'Compliment charts' where teachers can write praise and encouragement – this is often found in a homework diary.
- Telephone calls or notes home that commend good behaviour.

Getting Out

88 I've had enough!

Teaching isn't the dream job for everyone who decides to give it a try. Although official figures are rather varied, general research in the field suggests that between 40 per cent and 60 per cent of teachers leave the profession within the first three years. This includes student teachers and NQTs. Some studies go so far as to claim that more than one in three leave within their first five years, often citing workload pressures, stress and long working hours as reasons for their departure.

Although the British government has tried multiple incentives to encourage graduates to join the teaching profession, if the figures are to be believed, many newly qualified teachers would prefer working in a call centre to a school!

 Be aware: everyone gets dissatisfied or disappointed with their job sometimes. Making the decision to leave the profession is not something you should do hastily. Give yourself the time to think things through properly and draw up a list of personal pros and cons. It might be better to consider a change of school rather than leaving the profession entirely.

If you do decide to leave your current position, bear in mind that you will need to give plenty of notice – usually a full half term. For example, if you wish to leave at Christmas, you must have handed in your notice by the end of October. This will give your employer plenty of time to find someone to replace you, and your classes are not disrupted by suddenly having a new teacher halfway through a term.

In some situations, the school may decide to let you leave early. This may be the case if you are obviously unhappy in your position: it is more beneficial for the school to find a teacher who isn't a nervous, emotional wreck!

Any teacher who is contemplating leaving the profession should contact their union for advice and support. Your union representative will not try to change your mind, but they will go over all the possible options for you. If you are an NQT it is advisable to complete your induction year, or at the very least a full term, in case you decide to return to teaching after a break. If you are a student teacher, you may wish to take a short break (up to four terms) between achieving QTS and beginning your induction.

Remember: you will never lose your PGCE or QTS qualification once you have earned it.

All NQTs are expected to complete their induction within five years, although this does not have to be in consecutive terms. If you are finding your induction year a struggle, you might find it better to tackle each term in stages, or even at different schools. You can teach in private schools, as a private tutor or overseas without ever having to complete your induction period.

Teaching can get very tough, but it is also incredibly rewarding. Always make sure you put any problems in perspective – you made it through your training year and passed your QTS tests, not to mention survived on a student teacher's salary for nine months: you are probably a lot stronger than you think!

My NQT year was incredibly difficult. To be honest, I picked the wrong school for me. I had very few problems during my training, but my induction seemed to be fraught with stresses and problems. Every night I went home miserable, and I could hardly drag myself out of bed the next day. Eventually I decided I had had enough and, after talking it over with friends and family, I decided to hand in my notice. I left at Easter after successfully completing two terms of induction and took a break for a while. I returned to teaching in the September at a completely different school and it has been amazing. I have rediscovered my love of teaching once more and I have been teaching for nearly four years. It just proves that often it's not your teaching ability that is the problem, but that you need to pick the right school that will give you the support you need.

Jake, Physics teacher (28)

89 Changing schools successfully

Leaving one school to join another can be easy or hard, depending on what kind of changes you're making and where you are in your career. As a new teacher, finding a new job might not be as daunting an experience as for someone who has held the same position for 20 years. This is because, although you may not have the same level of professional experience, you are quite used to going from school to school, as you did during your training and induction year.

The process of searching and applying for a new teaching job is pretty much the same in all schools. Once you have found an opening, either through scouring the local job papers, the *TES* or the Internet, you will need to make an outstanding application. In some areas, closing schools and low staff turnaround can mean as many as 60 applicants may go after one position. It is advisable to check out the competition thoroughly before you quit your current position.

In addition to an excellent application form, you will need at least two glowing references. Some schools will only ask for a reference once you have been shortlisted for the post, or offered the job. This can be useful if you plan to change jobs without letting your current workplace know straight away.

One of your referees should be your current manager, but the other may be from a different source entirely. Whoever you choose to supply your reference, always make sure you ask their permission and encourage them to highlight your skills and accomplishments.

 Remember: if you are offered the position, it may be a good six to eight weeks or more before you will actually start there, due to the term structures. If you are already working in a school, you must give plenty of notice if you plan to leave. If this is to be your first proper teaching job after your ITT, you may find it necessary to find temporary work to see you through the holiday weeks.

Although you won't start teaching until the term starts, most schools may expect you to spend at least a couple of days at the school before the students return. This will help you to familiarize yourself with the layout of the school, prepare any initial lessons, organize your classroom and meet your new colleagues.

As in any new job, you should expect some form of induction process to take place to ensure you fit into the school system with as little fuss as possible. You should expect to be introduced to some members of senior management, your Head of Department or Faculty and your immediate department colleagues. You should also be told other essential details such as where the toilet facilities are located, how to find the staffroom and lunchtime arrangements!

Although you cannot expect to fit in immediately, try your best to meet as many new people as you can, and hopefully make a few friends. Whatever impression you want to give, always be yourself. Within a few weeks you should feel like you are a part of the school and (hopefully) are an essential part of the team.

90 But I haven't had an interview in 15 years!

Some teachers stay in the same school for so long they practically become a part of the decor. Others may stay for a considerable period of time before deciding to move onwards and upwards in their career. Yet more may jump from school to school every year until they find a place where they are happy to settle. However long you stay in your current position, and regardless of how many interviews you may have had throughout your career, once you have decided to test the waters elsewhere, it is essential you prepare.

Many interviews for teaching positions can last the whole day. You will be given a tour of the school and an introduction and welcome from the Headteacher. In addition to the actual interview you may be asked to teach an example lesson, observe a class, and meet with potential new colleagues. Most schools will decide who is the successful candidate that day, but you may have to wait a bit longer before you find out how you fared.

It is often impossible to find out what a school is really like until you actually start teaching there. However, during the interview process, if you feel that the role or the school does not meet your expectations, don't be afraid to retract your application and pull out of the interview process. After all, it is important you feel comfortable in the school you work for.

The questions you will be asked in the actual interview will depend on the type of school or position you are applying for. Always do some background research into the school and consider what kind of person they are likely to look for.

Typical questions you may be asked in an interview

- Why did you decide to become a teacher?
- What attracted you to this position?
- What kind of teacher do you consider yourself to be?
- What kind of qualities do you think you will bring to this role?
- How do you encourage students to learn?
- How would you handle a student who seems gifted, but presents a discipline problem?
- Describe a lesson that you feel was particularly successful and tell us why.

- How do you differentiate your teaching for SEN or G&T students?
- How do you establish authority/discipline?
- How do you react when a discipline problem arises?

Be prepared for the opportunity to ask your own questions. If you need to, write them down beforehand. This will show any prospective employer how prepared you are and how serious you are about gaining the position.

 Remember: in all interviews it is crucial to sell yourself. Never be afraid to talk about your skills and accomplishments – be proud of what you have achieved. You are the product that you want a prospective employer to buy: make sure you look and sound professional, motivated and determined from the very first moment you meet them.

91 Getting good references

When you decide to move on, either to another teaching job or to a completely different profession, you are going to need at least two references from your previous employers to support any job applications. For most, this is a simple process of asking your senior management or Head of Department to write a reference detailing your skills and achievements – but for others, there may be obstacles in the way.

Not everyone has a great time at the school they chose to work in: perhaps illness or other factors have affected your attendance, or you didn't get on with your senior management. Some people decide to change their career direction and aren't sure how their teaching skills will be relevant to their newly chosen path.

References should ideally come from people who have been responsible for overseeing your work, but you can also choose to include a personal or 'character' reference. Some employers will merely pass on the facts of your employment: job title, length of employment, salary and amount of time off you have had. This can be frustrating for you, especially if you know they could comment on some of your best working achievements, but it really will depend on your school's policy.

 Be aware: legally, your employer cannot give you a bad reference – i.e. they cannot submit a reference that is defamatory or will adversely affect your chances of employability. They can, however, make a negative statement providing it is in 'good faith'. For example, if your employer is asked about your time-keeping skills, which have been poor, they are well within their rights to inform prospective employers of the facts.

Common sense works well when it comes to references. You should contact the potential referee directly, ask their permission to use them as a reference and ensure you have known the person long enough. If possible, you could discuss your career goals and expectations with them, so that they have an idea of what to write on your behalf. If you are hoping to progress in your career, or to try something new, tell them this, so they can help to make your current skills relevant to your application. If you are really lucky, you might even get to see the reference before it is sent off.

92 Should I stay or should I go?

 Be aware: warning – do not let this calamities put you off teaching! If you are looking for reasons to 'justify' your decision to leave, you will find them here, but always remember to put things into perspective.

The best reason to stay in teaching is because you are passionate about your job and gain real satisfaction out of what you do. The worst reason is because of the salary.

Many teachers stay in the profession for a long time, and some become embittered and cynical, which shows in their teaching. Younger teachers often burn themselves out by taking on too much or finding it hard to deal with the workload pressures.

There are hundreds of different reasons why you might want to jack it all in and never look back. However, if you don't want to end up becoming another teaching 'drop out' statistic, the following checklist should help you decide if you should stay put and stick it out, or get out while you can. If you can answer an honest 'yes' to more than three of these questions, it might be time to consider a change.

1   Do you feel constantly tired, anxious or stressed while you are at work, and honestly believe this is due to your job?
2   Are you struggling to keep up with the workload pressures and feel you cannot cope with what is expected of you?
3   Have you found yourself treating students differently, perhaps being unnecessarily stern or aggressive without good cause?
4   Have you become disillusioned with the education system, curriculum requirements or even just teaching in general?
5   Do you feel you would be better suited to employment elsewhere, preferably out of the education sector?

6   Is your salary the *only* reason you stay in your job?
7   Do you find that you spend more time concentrating on the negative sides to the job than enjoying it?
8   Do you feel your job is having a negative impact on your home and/or family life, or has taken over your life too much?
9   Has your GP prescribed you medication, or have you turned to any drugs or stimulants to help you 'cope' with the stresses of your job?
10 Is it the case that when you are asked to list the things you enjoy about your job, you honestly can't think of any?

This checklist makes teaching look bleak and disheartening, but it is important to remember that the profession doesn't have to be like that. You may find that a change of school is the best thing for you, or perhaps you just need to take a short break for a while to reassess your career.

 Remember: when you are stressed or worried, it is easy to convince yourself that things are far worse than they are. For a list that shows why teaching is a fun and enjoyable profession, see Calamity 96.

93 What not to say when you leave

So you've decided to go, there has been a whip-round for you, and now you are expected to make some sort of speech in front of the other staff. You might not have had a great time at your particular school, but now is not the time to bad mouth anybody!

Speeches should last no more than around five minutes, and should ideally be brief, witty and praise other colleagues. Appeal to 'teacher humour' and give your thanks to those you have worked with. Avoid too many 'in-jokes' or any direct criticism of students or staff members.

Tips for a good leaving speech

- Keep it short.
- Make it witty – use a couple of jokes or funny one-liners to raise a chuckle.
- Summarize some of your best moments – as well as an embarrassing one if you're feeling daring!
- Thank your colleagues for their support and tell them that you will miss them and the school very much.

For some teachers, the prospect of leaving the school may feel like they are getting out of jail! Even if you really cannot wait to get out of those school gates, try to curb your enthusiasm. After all, you may need to call on your ex-colleagues in the future for references!

What not to say (real examples!)

The following are real quotes from leaving speeches made by teachers at various schools. It is safe to say that these teachers had fallen into the 'bitter and twisted' category!

'I wish I could say I was sorry to leave, but I'm afraid I'm not a liar, and I have to say I'll be glad to see the back of this place.'

'This school used to be a wonderful place to work; what a shame the current management changed all that.'

'Frankly, anyone who stays here out of choice needs their head examining!'

'I've been teaching for 17 years, and now, finally, I am going to a job where I will actually feel valued.'

94 I've done my time

Normal retirement age for teachers is 60, for both men and women. However, it is not unusual for many teachers to take early retirement if they can. After all, who really wants to be coping with the stresses and workload of full-time teaching past middle age?

The Teachers' Pension Scheme (TPS) has a variety of flexible options for teachers who decide to 'step down' or leave the profession completely, but do make sure you have checked out your entitlements and obligations before you decide to leave.

 Be aware: if you are leaving due to ill health, you will be entitled to incapacity benefits through the pension scheme, providing the DfES medical advisor is satisfied that you are permanently incapacitated.

Many older teachers find it beneficial to reduce their workload and teach part-time until they retire, providing they can earn enough to contribute to their pension. Teachers may also return to teaching employment after retirement without adversely affecting their pension, but they must discuss this with the TPS before accepting the appointment.

If you do decide to retire early, you must be prepared to make your application in good time. Most teachers retire at the end of school term or year, i.e. 31 December, 30 April or 31 August. You should submit any retirement applications at least three months before the date you plan to leave.

Although you may be looking forward to retirement with great glee, many retired teachers also complain that after all their years of teaching, they have nothing to do! Some ex-teachers find this to be a blessing and enjoy their well-earned rest, while others still continue to be an active part of the education sector, either voluntarily or through local schemes.

 Remember: whatever you decide to do during retirement, make sure you enjoy yourself. Someone who teaches all of his or her life could potentially clock up nearly 40 years of teaching experience. That's a long time to be in a classroom!

95 Other things to do with a teaching qualification

A teaching qualification doesn't limit your job prospects to just teaching. Don't forget, you have a professional qualification in a respected profession, not to mention a whole host of other skills you may have picked up during your teaching experience.

In addition to your in-depth subject knowledge, you will also have a number of key skills, including the following:

- Effective communication and leadership
- Organization and planning
- People management (for a variety of age ranges)
- Independence and motivation
- Practical IT, literacy and numeracy skills
- High standards and expectations

Leaving classroom teaching does not mean you have to leave your professional vocation behind: you may wish to branch out into specialist educational fields or become a tutor or adult educator. The following are some examples of other popular professions that many ex-teachers choose:

- Training and consultancy
- Individual tutoring or lecturing for other education sectors (not just schools)
- Counselling and mentoring
- Examination Boards or Local Education Authority inspection work (e.g. OfSTED representatives)
- Publishing or writing (usually specifically for the education market)
- Information Technology (hardware and software) professions
- Careers advice or youth work (e.g. Connexions)
- Museums, library and information work
- Teaching English as a Foreign Language, or Life Skills tutoring for adults
- The Armed Forces

Staying Put

96 Why teaching is fun

Teaching is a stimulating, exciting and challenging career that can bring a real sense of purpose to your working life. It can be difficult, stressful and sometimes very draining, but there is no doubt that teaching is a special and unique career.

Reasons why teaching is brilliant

- It is exceptionally rewarding and entertaining – no two days are ever really alike, and you are constantly challenged in numerous ways. Teaching is never dull!
- You get to work with young people every day to make a real impact and difference to their lives. Working with young people will keep you feeling young too!
- You will work with like-minded people who are also enthusiastic and passionate about their jobs and who share your sense of purpose.
- You will be part of a respected and secure profession where you have excellent opportunities to progress and expand.
- You can work pretty much anywhere in the world if you want to. Although job competition is fierce in some areas, teachers are in constant demand.
- You will earn a reasonable salary, which increases as you gain more experience or are promoted.
- Officially, you only have to work 195 days a year!
- Although you do have to conform to National Curriculum expectations, ultimately you have control over how and what to teach.
- It is likely to be the most satisfying and life-changing job you will ever do.

97 Reasons why you teach – it's not just the pay cheque!

By now you may be tired of reading all these excellent reasons why you should teach. You might even be looking at the title of this book and thinking, 'But this book is telling me about the possible calamities I might experience as a teacher. Why would I want to teach in the first place?'

The following are the frank and honest opinions of some real teachers in response to the question, 'Why are you a teacher?'

To be honest, I became a teacher by accident. After spending a few years in various uninspiring jobs I decided to go back to university to study a PGCE and train for a real career. I didn't feel especially passionate about teaching, but I had a good upper second degree in Mathematics, and I quite enjoyed working with children. The training year was very hard, and I found the course requirements very demanding – particularly the essay writing! Being in the schools was the easy bit, and I found that I really seemed to get on with the students. I managed to get my first job in one of the schools I did my training at, so I already had a good understanding of how the school worked, and knew the staff. I've been teaching at the same school for four years now and have steadily progressed up the ladder. It's still a very time-consuming and sometimes stressful job, but I can't imagine doing anything else.

Malcolm, Mathematics teacher (32)

Since leaving university in 1979, I have worked in IT, telecommunications and financial support. As I grew older I decided I wanted a job that would really stimulate and challenge me. I had considered teaching back when I was a graduate, but ended up taking a different career path. I enquired about teacher training and decided to do the work-based training route that meant I could train while working, as well as earning an income. I worked as an unqualified teacher for a year before gaining my QTS. I now teach IT to post-16 students at a special technology college, which is loads of fun.

James, ICT teacher (49)

I lived and taught in South Africa for nearly 15 years before relocating to England to be near my family. My father was a teacher and loved his work immensely, which I believe inspired me to follow the same career path. Initially I decided to take a break from teaching, but after a few months I realized I missed the diversity and pleasure that teaching provided me with.

I decided to teach secondary English, but despite all my teaching experience I still had to meet certain standards to gain QTS. I secured a position in a local school and contacted the TDA for advice. I am now working through a Registered Teacher Programme, which allows me to work and train while studying for QTS.

Anita, English teacher (44)

I wanted to be a teacher for as long as I could remember. As a child I used to 'teach' my toys and turn my bedroom into a classroom. After finishing my A-levels, I decided to take a Bachelor of Education course, which would mean I could teach primary school children. It took me four years to complete the course, and I gained QTS in addition to my degree. I have been teaching at a primary school for almost two years and it's my dream job. Most of my friends think I'm mad, but it really is such a rewarding profession.

Julie, Primary teacher (25)

98 Having a successful career

There are four key stages to a teacher's professional development:

1 Initial teacher training – PGCE/GTP/BEd, etc.
2 The induction process – the first/NQT year of teaching.
3 Early professional development (EPD) – the second and third years of teaching.
4 Continuing professional development (CPD) – beyond three years of teaching.

After the initial stresses of training, induction and your early teaching years, the job does start to get a lot easier and less stressful. You may find that you 'recycle' lesson plans, your marking and planning sessions may become more straightforward, and you have learned to balance your home and working life much better. With everything going so well, it can be easy to slip into complacency.

 Remember: good teachers recognize that in order to progress, they must also be prepared to expand their learning. There will always be new challenges and opportunities open to you, and it is important you don't let them slip by.

Some positions will be available to you as you gain more teaching experience, such as becoming the Head or Assistant Head of a department, faculty, year or key stage. You will need to prove to your management that you have the relevant skills and experience for the role, but your prospects will be greatly improved the longer you have stayed in teaching.

You may consider applying for an Advanced Skills Teacher (AST) post. ASTs are exceptional teachers who spend at least 80 per cent of the time in the classroom, while devoting the other 20 per cent to other schools, such as working for community outreach programmes. AST posts are usually created by your Headteacher and funded through the Local Education Authority.

Be aware: before you apply for or accept any promotion, be sure it is what you want. Sometimes the increase in salary or 'status' can seem tempting, but ensure you know what the additional responsibilities will be. The further you move up the career ladder, the less time you will spend actually teaching and being with the students.

More money + more responsibility = more paperwork.

Assessing your career progression, at any point in your career, is a good way of making sure you are getting the most out of your job. Although there is no harm in getting comfortable, particularly if you have found a role that you are happy in, don't blinker yourself to other possibilities that may be open to you.

Teaching career progression checklist – Are you getting the best out of your job?

- Have you been given suitable opportunities to expand your skills and training?
- Have INSET and professional development days been useful and worthwhile in terms of improving your teaching skills?
- Has your career progressed within the last five years, or are you still in the same role you were originally hired to do?
- Does your school/Local Education Authority take Continuous Professional Development for teachers seriously?
- Are you encouraged to expand your skills and experience, and do you feel valued in your job?
- Are you encouraged to build a career portfolio of your skills and achievements?
- Are you given the opportunity to discuss your career progression plans with senior management, and do they support and encourage you?

99 Additional training for all teachers

Every teacher can benefit from continuous professional development (CPD) opportunities, to gain essential ongoing training and support throughout their teaching careers. Although in-service training (INSET) and professional development days will be provided by your employer, ultimately it is your responsibility to ensure your career is progressing as you want it to.

If you wish to expand your academic skills, you may wish to consider further study at postgraduate level. You can combine teaching and research-based work and build on your previous qualifications while studying for a Master's degree (MA/MSc/MEd). This will also help you advance your knowledge and understanding in an academic context. Some employers will even help fund your Master's course. The Training and Development Agency for Schools (TDA) can advise you on any CPD queries you may have. Visit their website at www.tda. gov.uk for more information.

There are 'Fast Track' routes available to teachers in the early stages of their careers, which allow them the opportunity to study and train for a leadership role. The Fast Track aim is to equip teachers with the necessary skills they need to be ready for leadership roles within five years. See www.fasttrackteaching.gov.uk for more details.

If you already have a lot of teaching experience and good qualifications, you may be considering moving into headship. The National College for School Leadership (www.ncsl.org.uk) can advise you on headship and senior management programmes.

Most schools will have a designated notice board in the staffroom where you will find details of any upcoming local courses and professional development opportunities. Don't be afraid to ask about further training opportunities if you believe they will be useful to you.

 Remember: you can expand your skills and qualifications in a variety of ways, not just through those tailored specifically for teachers. For example, qualifications in mentoring or counselling can be particularly useful to those who want to work with troubled or 'difficult' children.

Teachernet, a government-supported website for teachers, has a huge section full of information on CPD. Visit www.teachernet.gov.uk/professionaldevelopment for more details.

Conclusion: So, you still want to be a teacher?

For many, the initial teacher training experience is a real 'sink-or-swim' test. Although teaching has the benefit of being surrounded by some excellent support networks, you do have to be directly responsible for your own career.

Many older teachers seem to have forgotten what it is like to be a newcomer, and because of this have adopted a harsher attitude when supporting young teachers. Their approach is often akin to 'If you can't stand the heat, get out of the kitchen'. If you have managed to get through your training and your induction without letting this, or any other negative viewpoints put you off, you should be very proud of yourself. If you're one of those older teachers who uphold these rather harsh views, try to think back to how you may have felt at the beginning of your career, and 'cut some slack'. It is worth remembering that teachers who work together as part of a team are ultimately happier, less stressed and deliver better quality lessons – so always support each other!

The reason teaching stands out from other jobs is because the role is so varied and stimulating. No two days are ever really alike, and you would be hard pushed to describe a 'typical' day. There is no doubt that teaching demands a lot of your time and attention. It is certainly not one of the easiest professions to work in, but that is a crucial part of its appeal. To be a successful and accomplished teacher you must be dedicated, motivated, prepared to work hard, and willing to accept a challenge. While there *is* a lot of planning, marking and assessing to do, you also have the opportunity to work with many different and vibrant young people, helping to have a positive impact on their lives.

The more effort you put into teaching, the more satisfaction you will get out of it. It is an excellent and unique career choice. Enjoy yourself!

A Few More Classroom Calamities

Control, Alt, Delete – Trouble with technology

With more and more teachers being encouraged to use ICT in the classroom, it is a good idea to familiarize yourself with at least the basics of ICT and teaching. While some teachers will happily integrate interactive whiteboards and PowerPoint demonstrations into their lessons, other teachers break out into a cold sweat when asked merely to turn on a PC.

The most important thing to remember is that the technology is designed to help you, not to trip you up. Whatever you may think, computers do not have a life of their own – they will (usually) only do what you tell them to do!

However, sometimes, regardless of how carefully you have planned your lesson, things will, and do, go wrong.

'My mouse ain't working, Sir' and other computer catastrophes

- When working with PCs, always have some kind of back-up plan. Whenever you plan to use technology in your lessons, always anticipate the worst.
- Make sure *you* are comfortable with the technology you are going to use: while using an interactive whiteboard seems like a great idea, if you don't know how to use it then your lesson will go down the pan.
- Where possible, check with your IT department if they know of any immediate IT issues that may disrupt your lesson: for example, if the network has gone down, the PCs are being upgraded, or the printer is broken.
- If your students need a password to log on to school computers, try to make sure you have a list of these available. Most students are very aware of how much lesson time they can waste just because they allegedly cannot log on to a PC.
- Keep a paper-based lesson plan handy just in case. Never just abandon a lesson because the computers don't work or something has gone wrong.

- Always highlight the importance of saving and backing up your work. Make sure students have saved their work properly, and where possible take a copy on the network, USB pen drive or even a floppy disk.

Ten ideas for getting students to use computers in lessons

PC's are not just for typing out coursework or checking emails. There are lots and lots of ways teachers can integrate PC use into their lessons. Here are just a few ideas.

1 Plan, design and publish a newspaper, magazine or leaflet.
2 Teach information literacy skills and encourage proper use of search engines, key words and website evaluation.
3 Create an interactive quiz and let students 'research' the answers online.
4 Prepare a multimedia presentation, such as a television-style advert.
5 Make music – use computer software to write a song or 'jingle', or be a DJ for the day.
6 Create a website for the class or the school and allow all students to contribute their ideas.
7 Re-write a piece of Shakespearean text in 'net-speak'.
8 Set up a 'video conference' to practise modern foreign languages.
9 Scan images and digitally manipulate or edit them.
10 Take advantage of teaching and learning based websites such as those produced by the BBC or the *TES*, or learn.co.uk

Big Brother is watching: Computer rules

Just because your school has access to the Internet does not mean you can spend your lunch hour browsing on the web – at least not if your browsing habits contravene your schools Internet usage policy.

Most schools have some form of Acceptable Use Policy for computer and Internet use, but this is frequently aimed at the students. In addition to signing a contract outlining your terms and conditions of employment, you may also be required to sign an additional document that outlines acceptable use of the Internet and email within the school.

According to the Department of Trade and Industry's Information Security Breaches Survey (ISBS), the two biggest areas of Internet misuse were excessive personal emails and accessing inappropriate websites. It is alleged that one in five companies has sacked an employee for inappropriate Internet use, and some frequently monitor staff emails. This includes schools, colleges and other education providers.

Internet Usage Policies may vary in length and description, but it is essential you are aware of what they say and mean. The following is a very basic example of what may be stipulated.

Internet Usage

1   The Internet service is provided to staff as a business and learning tool. Staff may use the Internet for non-school use providing this use is limited, occasional and not detrimental to their job or colleagues.
2   It is an offence to knowingly access any web sites with sexual or pornographic material, or any sites that promote or encourage racism, intolerance or any other objectionable material
3   Staff should not download any material from the Internet without prior consent and authorization from the IT Manager.
4   The IT department can monitor Internet usage cross-school at any time. Any abnormal or unacceptable Internet usage will be investigated. The IT department may record any unacceptable Internet use by staff and these records may be used as evidence in the event of a disciplinary.

5   The use of 'Anonymizer Websites' to mask browsing activities/prevent IT monitoring is not permitted. Staff who use anonymizer sites will be considered to be accessing unacceptable web content and may be subject to further investigation.

Email policy

1   Staff may use email for very occasional, limited, non-business use providing this is not detrimental to their job or colleagues.
2   All emails sent should be of a lawful content and must not include defamatory or libellous statements.
3   Any emails sent from the school's email address must uphold the reputation of the school and should include an appropriate notice and disclaimer.
4   Emails should not include any offensive comments based on an individual's gender, age, sexuality, race, disability or appearance.

Be especially aware of any 'joke' emails that you may be tempted to forward to friends or colleagues, especially if you use your school email address. Apart from potentially offending someone, you may find yourself at the centre of a disciplinary for misconduct.

 Remember: to put it simply, don't do *anything* on a school-based computer or Internet connection that you wouldn't feel happy about showing to everyone.

First aid and accidents

It would be very naive to think that throughout your teaching career you will never be faced with some sort of first aid emergency. Whether this is a simple nosebleed, a bang to the head from a football in PE or a more serious diabetic or epileptic fit, it is advisable to be prepared.

Under Health and Safety obligations, first aid provision must be available at all times while people are on school premises or on school-based trips. In the majority of schools the Local Education Authority and board of governors are responsible for organizing a first aid policy in schools.

Usual teaching terms and conditions do not include first aid duties, although any teacher may volunteer to undertake these duties. All members of staff are expected to use their best endeavours at all times to ensure the safety and well-being of students, particularly in emergency situations.

 Be aware: any officially appointed first aider must have completed a training course approved by the Health and Safety Executive (HSE). Any member of staff may be an appointed person, or someone who takes charge when someone is ill or injured. Appointed persons do not need to have HSE approved training, although it is recommended that they have some appropriate first aid training. Appointed persons should not give any form of first aid that they have not been trained to do.

If you do not have any first aid knowledge, consider a short course with St John's Ambulance. If any of your students are known to have any specific medical needs, it is advisable that you gain some basic knowledge, which will help you deal with any medical emergencies.

Basic first aid tips

- Assess the situation – do not put yourself in any danger – make the area safe.
- Assess all casualties – attend to unconscious casualties first.
- Send for help immediately.

Unconscious casualties

If a person does not respond to gentle shaking of the shoulders and shouting, they may be unconscious. Your priority is to check their Airway, Breathing and Circulation (the **ABC** of resuscitation).

1 Open the airway by gently tipping the casualty's head back. Remove any obvious obstruction.

2 Check if the casualty is breathing by looking at the chest and feeling and listening at the mouth.

3 If the casualty is breathing, put them in the recovery position and send or wait for help.

4 If the casualty is not breathing, begin to administer mouth-to-mouth resuscitation.

5 Check for signs of circulation: normal breathing, coughing or movement. If there are no signs of circulation, start chest compressions immediately.

6 Once the casualty begins breathing, place them in the recovery position and wait for help.

The recovery position

- Turn the casualty onto their side.
- Open their airway and place their hand under their cheek.
- Bring their leg upwards to ensure they cannot roll backwards or forwards.
- Continuously monitor their breathing and circulation.

Severe bleeding

- Apply direct pressure to the wound.
- Where possible, raise and support the injured part.
- Apply a firm bandage.

Broken bones

A qualified medical official should attend to all broken bones. If a spinal injury is suspected, you *must not* move the casualty unless they are in great danger.

Shock

Symptoms of shock include:

- Pale face
- Cold, clammy skin
- Shaking
- Rapid, weak pulse
- Fast, shallow breathing
- Unconsciousness

Shock is a medical emergency and should be treated very seriously.

- Reassure the casualty and keep them as calm as possible.
- Lie them down and raise and support their legs.
- Keep them warm with a blanket or coat.
- Do not give them anything to eat or drink.*
- Monitor their breathing and circulation.

* The symptoms of a diabetic hypoglycaemic episode (hypo) are very similar to those of medical shock. If you are certain that the casualty is suffering from a hypo, you may administer some form of glucose, such as a sugary drink.

Nosebleeds
- Sit the casualty down and reassure them.
- Pinch the tip of the nose, *not* the bridge.
- Do not tilt the head back – if necessary, put a bowl or other object in front of the casualty to catch any dripping blood.